MARATHONING: A BOOK
BY MANFRED STEFFNY

MARATHONING: A BOOK
BY MANFRED STEFFNY
Translated by
George Beinhorn

ANDERSON WORLD, INC.
Mountain View, California

Recommended Reading:
Runner's World magazine, $16.00/year
Box 366, Mountain View, CA 94042
Write for a free catalog of publications
and supplies for runners and other athletes.

Library of Congress Cataloging in Publication Data

Steffny, Manfred, 1941-
    Marathoning.

    Translation of Marathontraining.
    1. Marathon running. I. Title.
GV1065.S7313   796.4'26   78-64388
ISBN 0-89037-156-3

Originally published 1977
by Verlag Dr. Hanns Krach, Mainz, W. Germany

Second Printing June 1980
Third Printing May 1981

Anderson World
Mountain View, CA

Contents

Foreword

I consider running—distance running in particular—the healthiest of all contemporary sports. The marathon is not the most arduous sport, as it's commonly known, but the most perfect sport for the human organism. Muscle elasticity, commitment of will, and preparation of the nervous system are all required in a single long run. The ability to recover from stress— not in an armchair, but while actually running—is equally important. The person who can put all these abilities together is a hero, who can rightly congratulate himself on the achievement. Medal or not, such a runner has proved his mettle.

This book on marathoning is a handbook for healthy, joy-filled, happy living as well. Marathoning goes beyond mere technical advice to show how to appreciate the abilities of your own body. It shows, too, that regardless of your age, you need never speak of "growing old." If you're looking for happiness in life or for a feeling of joy, you'll find the formula in this book. Happiness isn't something you go out and seek; but it's often a by-product of perspiration. When you exercise, the physical difficulties and stress of daily life begin to disappear. I hope that you are able to make a good effort and then to relax and look back happily on your performance.

Olympic Memories

The marathon has around it a halo of deep, symbolic meaning. It began with the ancient Greek hero in the fields of Marathon. But the first modern Olympic Games of 1896—in which the marathon was the high point—were just as heavy with symbolism as the old Greek legend. Once again, a Greek, Spiridon Louis, played the central role, and won the race, reviving the old legend. The story of Spiridon was followed in 1908 by tragedy: Italy's Dorano Pietri was just yards from the finish when his strength ran out and he collapsed.

But there were to be happy endings. In 1924 in Paris, Finland's Alfin Stenroos won and then, out of sheer joy, continued running until he reached the Olympic Village. In 1932 at Los Angeles, tragedy struck again. Paavo Nurmi had entered the race as a clear favorite, but was not permitted to start. He watched from the sidelines giving split times. The Argentinian runner, Juan Zabala, won and returned in 1936 in search of another gold medal. Despite high temperatures, Zabala went out at a fast pace and led for 22 miles. Then he faded as a new marathoning star rose: Kitei Son, a Japanese runner, who ran the first sub-2:30 race.

World War II ended an era. In 1948 at London, Gailly of Belgium entered the stadium a full third of a mile ahead of the second-place runner. Suddenly he stumbled and fell, unable to rise again and run. The stadium was as quiet as a cemetery. Gailly rose slowly and moved unsteadily toward the finish line just 250 meters away. The Argentinian, Delfo Carbrera, entered the stadium and passed Gailly to win the race. Not a soul cheered, for Gailly was still in mortal danger. Richards of England finished second, still to no applause. Gailly finally staggered past the finish line, third.

In those early days as a runner, I was forever aware of a shadow following close behind me. Alain Mimoun of France was forever finishing second in races that I won—in the 1952 Olympics and at the 1950 European Championships. One might well imagine that this man would have no love for me, but it was not so. In 1956, Mimoun at last won the most beautiful medal of them all. The best runners were all at the start of the Olympic marathon that year. Suddenly Mimoun was the man of the hour. At the end of the race he stood waiting for several minutes while I struggled to finish sixth.

I thought, "Well, he's waiting to taste the satisfaction of being congratulated by me, who usually beats him." And what happened? Mimoun shouted, "Emil! I've just had a child in France—I'm a father!" So I congratulated the happy father on his new baby daughter. Alain Mimoun had waited to tell me that! (The child had actually been born a few days before, but the French team directors had kept the news from Mimoun so he would not become nervous. They told him at the finish line.)

Bikila Enters the Scene

Then began a fabulous era in the marathon. An exotic runner came to the Rome Olympics—a man whose running debut was beyond compare. At the starting line in the Pantheon Stadium in 1960 stood the barefoot runner, Abebe Bikila from Ethiopia, with the cobblestones of the Via Appica Antica blisteringly hot before him. His entry was contrary to international rules, which state that all entrants must wear shoes in the Olympic marathon. The Italians, who had fought in Ethiopia during World War II and had faced Ethiopian warriors wielding bamboo spears, were amused by Bikila.

The Ethiopians' Finnish coach, Nikkanen was not smiling, but he wasn't in the least bit intimidated. He knew how strong his runners were, and he told Bikila, "That runner over there is Rhadi. He knows how to run, so stick with him." Bikila did just that, following Rhadi, who was in front at 19 miles, but getting nervous. Rhadi was running hard, but this barefoot runner was still following. With the end of the race just 5,000 meters away, Nikkanen yelled to Bikila, "Go past him." Bikila ran to a clear victory. At the finish line, Bikila showed no signs of fatigue, and actually tried to continue past the Arch of Constantine, thinking he still had to run to the Pantheon Stadium. Abebe Bikila struck the world of marathoning like lightning.

For a while Bikila was in serious trouble at home in Ethiopia. In an uprising by the Imperial Guard against the reigning Negus, Abebe was implicated as a member of the guard, though the Negus later pardoned him.

In spite of an appendicitis attack just weeks before the 1964 Olympics, he ran brilliantly at Tokyo. Never had an Olympic marathon been run so fast, nor had a winner finished looking so fresh. Before the astonished eyes of the spectators and world wide television audience, he launched into a series of calisthenics on the field after the race.

At the 1968 Mexico Olympics, Bikila had to drop out with

knee trouble. Gaston Roelants, who'd won a pre-Olympic race the year before in Mexico, also had knee problems and didn't finish. But at least Bikila was able to console himself with the victory of a fellow Ethiopian, Mamo Wolde. In Munich, Frank Shorter won while Bikila watched the finish from a wheelchair. At least he had the satisfaction that his Olympic record remained unbroken.

Abebe Bikila, the natural runner and barefoot champion in a technological age, became in the end a victim of that age. An auto accident ended first his running and later his life. While injuries are rare in marathoning, the example of Abebe Bikila shows that in the modern world with its technology, motors, and mobility, misfortune is never far away. Running is many times healthier than driving or any of the other activities of modern man. It is the maker of legends.

—Emil Zatopek

Part One

All About the Marathon

Chapter 1

Taking the Myths Out of the Marathon

Marathoning is a relatively recent sport. It began with a letter that Michel Brial, a member of the Institute de France, wrote to Baron de Coubertin. Brial proposed to organize a re-creation of the historic marathon race from Marathon to Athens, with a valuable cup as the winner's prize. After some initial hesitation, Coubertin adopted Brial's idea, and the first modern marathon was held on April 10, 1896. This much, at least, is fact. But everything else that has been written about the marathon of classical antiquity—including the Greek messenger's fatal run from the battlefield at Marathon to Athens to proclaim a victory over the Persians—belongs to the realm of legend. Anecdotes were created by historians of the day to add a little spice to their accounts. The historian Herodotus, who wrote at the time of the battle in 490 B.C., says nothing about a messenger's fatal run. If there had been truth to that story, Herodotus, a skilled historian and shrewd storyteller, would never have deprived the Greeks of the tale.

The legend of the marathon runner first appears 560 years after the Greek battle, in the writing of the Roman historian Plutarch. The story aided Plutarch in making a colorful transition from the battlefield to the cosmopolitan city of Athens and its victory celebration. Like the other historians of antiquity, Plutarch was also a storyteller.

The Longest Distance?

Even the present standard racing distance of 26 miles, 385 yards is not historically correct. It is about 23.5 miles from the fishing village of Marathon to Athens. The present official race course from Marathon to Athens (standardized at the 1969 European Championships) ambles far to the left five kilometers from the start, alongside the graves of 192 of the Greeks who fell in battle with the Persians. This course was laid out in this way so it would cover the full 26 miles, 385 yards.

From 1896 to 1906, the distances varied. In 1908, the English princess wanted to watch the start of the race from her window in Windsor Palace and the finish from the stadium box. The princess' wish was the Olympic organizers' command, and the extended London course set the precedent for all future races. Runners since 1908 have owed the additional 1.36 miles to a princess' royal whim. Kind thoughts while running the last mile and a third may thus be properly addressed to Her Royal Highness.

Michel Brial's revival of the marathon accelerated the development of long road races, probably by decades. In nineteenth-century England it was not an unusual feat to run 25 or 26 miles in a race or while carrying messages; nor was it strange in other cultures of a hundred years ago. The fact that 26 miles has come to be considered the ultimate distance-running event is due almost entirely to the publicity surrounding this early modern marathon.

The Most Grueling Event?

Aside from the story of the Greek messenger's death, a number of other factors contribute to the stereotype of the marathon as a grueling event. One problem is that Olympic organizers have consistently and unreasonably scheduled the race start for midday. In addition, runners in the past were often poorly trained, as the marathon was a "second event" for many of them. The image of agony and death hardened to the level of a dogma when Italy's Dorando Pietri collapsed while in the lead, just before the finish of the 1908 Olympic marathon. One of the most widely published sports photos of all time shows Pietri's collapse. But we know now that it was not the distance that cut Pietri down, but rather the fact that he was doped. Years after the event, on his death bed, the Italian who'd been pitied by a generation of sports enthusiasts confessed that he had cheated.

The physical stresses of marathoning are more evenly distributed than in other sports like bicycle racing. The stresses are great, but in terms of muscular effort they fall below the average for many other sports. The marathon is probably less difficult than the 50-kilometer ski marathon, the 50-kilometer walk, or the 10,000-meter speed skating race. But running marathons does require greater effort than other disciplines that do not call for continuous, consistently high levels of exertion.

Do Marathon Runners Train the Hardest?

Marathoning formerly demanded the most intense training of all sports. While training standards have risen enormously in all other athletic events, marathon runners simply have not been able to increase training much beyond the traditional levels. The optimum, even for world-class runners is about three hours a day. Compared with the time other athletes train, this isn't much. World-class gymnasts and figure-skaters must train six to eight hours daily. Swimmers train four or five hours. Modern strength and conditioning methods—not required and possibly even harmful for marathon runners—are now indispensable for even middle-distance runners. As a result, middle-distance runners must actually train longer than marathoners. The varied workouts of weight lifters, decathletes, hammer-throwers, and shot-putters may look frightening to the marathoner putting in a relatively relaxed fifteen miles daily at an aerobic pace.

Good preparation and modern shoe design have significantly reduced the possibility of injury in marathon training. Recently many injured runners have turned from the track to road-racing because it doesn't hurt their legs so much. From an orthopedic point of view, the marathoner's running style is much healthier than, for instance, that of a triple jumper or a soccer player.

Marathon Man—Superman?

If society is awed by the marathon runner, this is due less to his actual performance than to the distance he runs. To gain a feeling for 26 miles, the average American figures out how long it would take him to drive that far. He then compares his elapsed time with that of the marathoner and discovers that the difference is less than he expected.

Marathon runners are the objects of considerable wonder. But instead of basking in the glow of others' admiration, it's more constructive to try and break down the myths that surround the sport so that more people will be encouraged to try running. As long as people drive to the corner mailbox, the diseases of inactivity will continue to spread. In countries where people still cover long distances on foot as our own grandfathers did, the marathon is looked on as quite natural. In Ethiopia, for example, people fall into an easy trot just to get to their destination a little faster. In such places distance running is the sport of the people. So it doesn't seem right for the marathon runner to allow himself to be labeled an outsider, an exception, or a freak.

Is the marathoner a man of high ideals? You meet this idea wherever you go, and it's about as far removed from reality as it is to call the marathoner a self-tortured masochist. Men jump, run, swim, or climb mountains not because of idealism, but to satisfy personal ambition or hunger for adventure, to awaken feelings of joy, to make friends, or to find themselves. So many things have been done in the name of idealism that one should guard against calling someone an idealist merely for running 26 miles.

Compared with billiards, bobsledding, sailing, and fencing, the marathon is a fairly normal thing to do. That is why it is practiced worldwide. It's more demanding than most other sports, and it is frequently misunderstood or distorted. The simple facts of the event are overlooked and sensationalized. The marathon belongs no more to the man of intense will and ambition than to the plodder without the natural gift of speed. It has its own internal laws, and tends to attract people of a certain mentality, just like any other sport.

Chapter 2

Distance Running, The New Mass Sport

In the mid-1960s Arthur Lydiard of New Zealand, Bill Bowerman of the United States, and Dr. Ernst van Aaken of West Germany led a sports movement that got people of the industrialized nations out of their easy chairs and onto the roads. These coaches preached running as an ideal path to fitness and sports participation for people of all ages. They focused on a variety of coaching interests that included both world-class athletes and the slowest beginners.

These three coaches, who drew their inspirations from coaching practice, share credit for the 1960s running boom with Dr. Kenneth Cooper, the laboratory physiologist. Cooper proposed fitness tests and running programs to help condition the average person for increased efficiency in all areas of his life. Cooper's accomplishments should not be underestimated. The eight million joggers in America in the sixties formed the broad base that spawned the marathon boom. America, the land of sprint, jump, and throw, suddenly had a number of exceptionally good marathoners. Frank Shorter, gold medalist at the 1972 Olympics and second in 1976; Bill Rodgers; and Kenny Moore are the cream of a burgeoning crop of marathoning talent. A decade ago, Europeans considered Americans too soft to run the marathon. Now America has the most sub-2:20 runners of any country in the world. There were 197 marathons held in the United States in 1977, and roughly 22,000 runners ran marathons that year. *Runner's World*, the magazine of distance running, has over 600,000 readers, making it the most widely circulated running magazine in the world.

9

Under the influence of Dr. van Aaken and the Association of Veteran Distance Runners that he founded, veterans' (over-forty) running has grown rapidly in Europe. Women's marathoning, another strong interest of van Aaken's, has developed rapidly around a nucleus of racing activity in the United States and West Germany. Children have been running the long distances in far greater numbers in the United States than in any other country, due in large part to the efforts of the Road Runner's Club of America.

Lydiard, Coach of the Coaches

If he'd been confined to his homeland of New Zealand, Arthur Lydiard would have had limited international influence. From the limited running potential of a country with just 2½ million inhabitants, Lydiard was able to discover and develop an extraordinary group of distance running stars, like Olympic champions Peter Snell, Murray Halberg, and John Walker, as well as a half-dozen other world-class runners.

Since Lydiard has served as coach for the national running teams of various countries, he has had a deep and enduring influence on the worldwide running scene. Lydiard was a prime influence in the Finnish running renaissance of Vaatainen, Viren, Vasala, Paivarinta, and Nikkari. He taught the coaches of champions how they should train their runners.

55,000 Milanese Can't Be Wrong

In my native West Germany, the field at the tradition-rich Black Forest Marathon has grown to 2,500. If you include the people who have earned the marathon certificate in our national fun-running programs and in privately sponsored fun-runs, there are about 8,000 active marathoners in West Germany. In 1976, 400 fun-runs were held in West Germany, with over 400,000 participants.

In other European countries, running has grown at a similar pace. The Italians have taken to running like hounds after the hare. In terms of the size of race fields, they stand unchallenged except by the United States. A marathon in Rome had 4,000 entries. The "Stramilano" half-marathon through the streets of downtown Milan holds the all-time record for entries in a distance run with 55,000.

All this running may surprise some observers, but it's a predictable symptom of advancing civilization and it's getting stronger. Distance running is not merely a reaction against the sedentary life-style, but is a reaction to the increasing loss of identity in jobs and modern life in general. We no longer identify ourselves with the way we earn our daily bread. As a result, we feel much closer to our hobbies.

"In reality, I'm a marathon-runner," says Erich Segal, bestselling author, professor of romantic languages, and accomplished pianist. Is it any wonder that thousands of others also think of themselves as marathoners first? And we are not referring to life's eternal losers. These are government officials, doctors, tax consultants, engineers, and scientists, all of whom have turned their attention to the Olympic racing distance most frequently associated with drudgery. No longer is marathoning dominated by farmers and laborers, the introverted but well-spoken intellectual is now the stereotypical marathon runner. And the marathon runner of today is less inspired by Coubertin's "higher, faster, farther" than by van Aaken's "slower, farther, and into a ripe old age."

A sociological phenomenon has grown with the marathon. There are two directions in modern sport, and they're becoming increasingly separated. On one hand, there are the few superstars chasing maximal performance and ignoring the cost in health damage. On the other hand, legions of health-conscious fitness buffs are developing highly individualized attitudes toward running, with the main emphasis on the quality rather than the quantity of the experience.

Real talent is being enticed away from the track and out onto the roads. The variety of racing and travel opportunities is more appealing, and winning against a dozen other runners on the track is not half as satisfying for a runner as beating a thousand others in a road race.

Chapter 3

Pacing Is the Key

Even pace is an essential factor in marathon racing. In no other sport will you gain so much from an ability to apportion your energy. Poor pacing, which usually involves starting too fast, can be disastrous. A few minutes advantage at the beginning of a race is all too frequently lost within the space of a couple of miles after the runner's energy reserves have dwindled.

A steady running rhythm, practiced in training, is just as important for the world-class runner as for the beginner; it outweighs all other tactical considerations. Sometimes during a race it may appear that a runner has made a winning breakaway at eighteen or twenty miles. But more likely this runner has paced himself well, and the others are now falling behind him.

Let's now talk about racing on a flat marathon course. A runner can predict his split times for the marathon on the basis of his best previous race time or his best time for 10,000 meters. He'll do well to run through his estimated splits as consistently as possible. Things, however, are more complicated if the course is rolling or hilly, or if there are weather changes like mid-day heat after a cool morning start, or sudden wind or rain. While you can make a fairly good estimate of the expected time losses for hilly sections of the course, winds can make predictions much more difficult.

Walter Weba, coach of the West German marathoners in international competition, wrote in 1972 that equal split times are less important than equal distribution of effort. In other words, the stopwatch is merely a way to keep your effort at a continuous level. The runner should definitely run faster with a trailing wind than against an opposing wind and faster down-hill than up; but most marathon courses are reasonably flat. The marathon pacing tables that follow should be a valuable pacing tool, since nearly all marathon courses are marked at five-mile intervals.

Pacing is especially important during the first half of the race, since a fast second half is the exception in the marathon. In the great international races, no matter how evenly a runner paces himself, a faster second half is impossible. The split times from Olympic Games races show that runners who led at the halfway mark in the race—as Frank Shorter did at Munich—have rarely gone on to win.

If a runner finds that he's able to go faster over the second half, he may delight in the fact. But it's also a sure sign that he would run a better overall race if he had gone out a little faster. The fastest split is usually the first five miles. It's generally impossible to pick up the pace past the fifteen- to eighteen-mile point. Accelerations between twenty and twenty-five miles are rare, and are a sign of extraordinarily good metabolic adaptation to the demands of the marathon.

Christa Vahlensieck's run at the 1977 German marathon championships in Berlin was a textbook case in marathon pacing. Christa had run 2:40 three times. Her good times had been run in unfavorable weather—heat in 1976, and heavy rain and cold earlier in 1977. But even pacing accounted for a good share in her enormous five-minute improvement in Berlin, to 2:34:47. Her rhythm was so finely-tuned that day that she didn't need to make even the slightest pace adjustments as she went through the five-kilometer checkpoints. Her split times were:

Distance	Race Time	Split Time
5 km.	18:55	18:55
10 km.	36:30	18:15
15 km.	54:40	18:10
20 km.	1:13:02	18:22
25 km.	1:31:20	18:18
30 km.	1:49:40	18:20
35 km.	2:08:15	18:35
40 km.	2:27:55	18:40

She couldn't have run at a more even pace. Here, too, the last five kilometers were the slowest. For most 2:20 runners, the last five-kilometer split is usually a full minute slower. In Christa's case the last split was just 20 seconds off the average. Even pacing accounted for her women's world-record time.

Chapter 4

Predicting Your Best Marathon Time

I've been fascinated with time-predicting systems since 1960, when I·first read a set of rules for predicting performances in a German book by Toni Nett. I was an age-group runner, and I'd been moving step by step from the 1,000 meters to longer races. As I ran each new distance, I found my best times corresponded exactly with those predicted by Nett's rules. Since I had good endurance, I was always able to make good use of my basic speed to fulfill my potential. This kept happening all the way up to 10,000 meters.

Here are Toni Nett's time-prediction guidelines:

1,500 meters	best-possible time is double best 800-meter time
3,000 meters	best-possible time is double best 1,500-meter time plus 20 seconds
5,000 meters	3,000-meter best time plus 20 seconds, times 5/3
10,000 meters	double best 5,000-meter time, plus one minute

Beyond this point, Nett's fountain of wisdom ran dry. For a long time, predicting marathon potential remained a closed book, as one might have expected in a day when marathon training was dismissed in running books with a few terse sentences. The running points tables of the International Amateur Athletic Federation (IAAF) only went up to 10,000 meters. Since I first become interested in the marathon, I've wanted to fill in these gaps. Naturally, my first desire was to discover my

17

own potential, then to train accordingly to realize my goals as a runner.

I scheduled by first marathon for the fall of 1967. My best time for 800 meters was 1:56.1, which had translated to a 1,500 in 3:52.0, a 5,000 in 14:09.0, and a 10,000 in 29:14.8. I was firmly convinced that these times were predictors of a similar level of success in the marathon. I threw into the formula my low running weight of 121 pounds, which hadn't helped at all in the middle distances, but which would provide a favorable power-to-weight ratio on the roads. I ran my first marathon in Berlin in 2:24:30.6, finishing ahead of the current German record-holder, Hubert Riesner, and felt I was on the path to a berth on the 1968 West German Olympic team.

My next goal was to run under 2:20, but my first attempt, on a muggy day, failed by half a minute. I resolved to run a season's best of 2:17—the time I'd arrived at after all kinds of calculations and plotting of curves. On the basis of physiological testing, Dr. van Aaken predicted the same time for me.

Shortly before the 1968 German national championships I had blood poisoning from a water blister on my foot and spent five days out of training, full of penicillin, and on my back in bed for part of the time. I nevertheless entered the championship race, but was forced to throw in the towel at twenty miles.

Dr. van Aaken energetically presented my case to the German Athletics Federation. He organized a race at Waldniel to select a runner for the third spot on the team for the Mexico Olympics. It was agreed that if I bettered the German record of 2:19:30, I could count on going to the Games. I went into the race full of cheeky confidence and won in a time of 2:17:13.8 in spite of heavy rain at the start. The two most dangerous opponents didn't show.

I'd gone into marathoning on a wing and a prayer to be sure, but sober calculations of running potential gave me confidence. Throughout the years I've collected best times for both world-class runners and plodders. It has been a challenge to piece together the training each individual used to run his best time. Eventually I drew up a table of marathon time predictions for the March 1975 issue of *Spiridon* magazine, which is reproduced here. My basic formula is:

marathon potential = 10,000-meter best time x 4.666

The numbers begin to deviate from the formula a little as times get faster, so I came up with another simple but accurate formula:

10,000 meters in 30 minutes = a marathon in 2:20

Differences of plus or minus one minute at 10,000 meters expand to plus and minus five minutes in the marathon. These are the maximum possible times. The best times of Frank Shorter, Lutz Philipp, Gunther Mielke, Paul Angenvoorth, Christa Vahlensieck, and even seventy-nine-year-old Arthur Lambert confirm these guidelines. There will always be discrepancies and difficulties in applying them, just as there are in attempting to apply Toni Nett's formulas. Ian Thompson, for instance, never races 10,000 meters at all and so can only give his 10,000-meter marathon splits as "best times." Derek Clayton, who apparently ran his 2:08:33 world record in Antwerp in 1967 on a short course, is another anomaly.

A runner specializing in either 10,000 meters or the marathon cannot fully realize his potential in the other. In the main, though, the table is a useful aid for marathon training and racing. In spring of 1975, for instance, I predicted a 2:40 for Christa Vahlensieck, knowing her 10,000-meter best was 34 minutes. My prediction was fulfilled.

It's interesting that the limits on endurance running times for men and women are the same. Maximal oxygen uptake and metabolism reveal only minor sex-specific differences. The limitations on performances at less than 10,000 meters imposed by women's bone structure and musculature merely present a somewhat slower basis for calculation. Speed losses, given equal training, are exactly the same as for men.

The figures I arrived at empirically were confirmed by research done in England by Dr. John Brotherhood, who used maximal oxygen uptake to formulate a relationship between 5,000-meter times and the marathon. He calculated that 80 to 90 percent of 5,000-meter speed is the predicted marathon pace. But most marathon runners neither realize their potential at 5,000 meters, nor are they even interested in running 5,000-meter track races; so Brotherhood's figures are less useful in practice. Applying Toni Nett's formula— 5,000-meter best time, times two, plus one minute—we find that Brotherhood is on the same wavelength as I was.

TABLE 1

Predicted Marathon Times

10,000 m. Best Time	Maximum Possible Marathon Time	Realistic Marathon Time
27:00	2:05:00	2:08:30
27:30	2:07:30	2:11:30
28:00	2:10:00	2:14:00
28:30	2:12:30	2:16:30
28:45	2:13:45	2:18:30
29:00	2:15:00	2:19:30
29:30	2:17:30	2:21:30
30:00	2:20:00	2:25:00
30:30	2:22:30	2:28:30
31:00	2:25:00	2:30:30
31:30	2:27:30	2:33:00
32:00	2:30:00	2:36:00
32:30	2:32:30	2:40:00
33:00	2:35:00	2:43:00
33:30	2:37:30	2:46:00
34:00	2:40:00	2:49:00
35:00	2:45:00	2:55:00
36:00	2:50:00	3:00:00
37:00	2:55:00	3:07:00
38:00	3:00:00	3:15:00
39:00	3:05:00	3:20:00
40:00	3:10:00	3:25:00
42:30	3:22:30	3:42:30
45:00	3:35:00	4:00:00
47:30	3:47:30	4:20:00
50:00	4:00:00	4:40:00

7.5　m　57
6　m　45.6
which is　7:31/mile

Chapter 5

History of Marathon Training

Without having always thought of what they were doing as a sport, men have always covered long distances by running. The legendary Greek messenger Pheidippides—called Aristidion in some sources—is supposed to have run 25 miles from Marathon to Athens and then fallen dead. This distance is short, however, when compared with other runs reported in classical antiquity. At the ancient Olympic Games, the longest racing distance was 24 lengths of the stadium, or 4,614.5 meters. An inscription at Epidauros says that Drymos, having won the victory at Olympia in the third century before Christ, ran all the way home to Epidauros to spread the news. Drymos would have run 87 miles. Ageus, an Olympic champion in 328 B.C., ran home 59 miles.

Early Runners

Foot messengers in Latin America have run much greater distances than the Greeks. The Tarahumara Indians of Mexico are now widely known for their days-long ritualized distance runs, which are still held. And the kath-carriers of Ethiopia still run some 11,000 miles a year with forty-pound loads of leaves of a type of narcotic.

Modern track and field began in England with distance running. It is reported that in 1653 an Englishman named Croydon ran twenty miles from St. Albans to London in less than an hour and a half. Since that time would be considerably faster than the present world record, this is not a reliable report. Thomas Calile's time of twenty-one miles in two hours in 1739 is more realistic.

In 1759, George Guest, also an Englishman, ran 1,000 miles in twenty-eight days. But his feat pales in comparison with Siegfried Bauer, a German emigrant living in New Zealand, who ran 1,000 miles in twelve days in South Africa. But Guest's time is astonishing for the century in which it was run. Among the running exploits of Foster Powell was a hundred-mile run in twenty-two hours in 1788. Englishmen discovered their love for the middle track distances in the early nineteenth century—possibly encouraged by the introduction of better timepieces and the faster tempo of life at the start of the Industrial Revolution.

With the inclusion of the marathon in the 1896 Olympic schedule, long-distance runs, hikes, and stage races began to crystallize in Europe around the new "historical" race. Just prior to the 1896 Games, a lightly built Greek army recruit was selected on the basis of his special toughness in long marches to represent his country in the Olympic marathon. To prepare himself, Spiridon Louis prayed for two days and fasted the day before the marathon. He won and in one stroke achieved world fame. Those who followed Spiridon Louis in the next few Olympic marathons made no special preparation either. In these races the dropout rate was high—not surprising since the race was usually started in the midday heat.

Because of the prestigious Boston Marathon (first held in 1897), marathon specialists first emerged in the United States. This resulted in gratifying wins at the 1904 Olympics by Thomas Hicks and by John Hayes in 1908.

Pihkala the Pacemaker

Not until the early 1920s did training for the long distances become a matter of precept and system. The Finns took command, as Paavo Nurmi ruled the world at all distances beyond 1,500 meters, and Hannes Kolehmainen ran an extraordinary time, for 1920, of 2:32:35.8 on an Olympic course too long by 555 meters. In 1924, Finland again won the marathon, with Albin Stenroos. It was coach Lauri Pihkala who had laid the cornerstones for the success of Nurmi and the other Finns. He was the first to develop a training system, and began training his runners years in advance of big meets.

Pihkala felt that an up-and-coming distance runner should begin preparing thirteen or fourteen weeks before the racing season. He laid out the following schedule:

- *First Period:* Two or three weeks of long walks at a moderate pace (20-30 miles for a marathoner), four or five times a week.

- *Second Period:* Two to three weeks of faster, but shorter walks 15-20 miles, four or five days a week. This included periods of easy jogging, and concluded with light calisthenics.

- *Third Period:* Three to four weeks of walking as in second period four or five days a week, but with easy forty- to seventy-meter sprints for 700 to 1,000 meters. Each sprint was followed by a slow run-down, and at the end of the workout a run of one to three kilometers.

- *Fourth Period:* Three to four weeks of daily morning walks, 10 to 12 miles. Three to five afternoons a week, he recommended cross-country and track running. Twice a week, long, slow cross-country runs for 7½ to 12 miles. The track work consisted of two to six laps for warm-up, followed by relaxed sprints of 70 to 120 meters for 15 miles.

- *Fifth Period:* During this period, the racing season, training was curtailed. In the morning there were easy walks, followed in the afternoon by interval-like track training and occasional runs at racing speed. At the first sign of overtraining, Pihkala recommended laying off for one week.

Between the racing season and the next training period Pihkala recommended a layoff of three or four months, during which the runner hiked or participated in other sports like boxing and soccer. Pihkala even felt that a break of a month or two from all sports activity was justified. The runner could allow himself to gain 5 to 10 percent in weight during that time, as long as he was not depleting his energy through dissipation. This period was for working or studying harder than usual, to strengthen the nervous system.

Fear of the Roads

Pihkala was horrified of road runs in training and coined the adage: "Marathon running is the horse cure for human legs, and the athletic swan song of former track stars." Pihkala saw the marathon as a running discipline for people over thirty and for those with little talent. Aside from the walking and running previously described, Pihkala placed great value on calisthenics and practicing style.

For tactics and running technique, Pihkala was a superb teacher, though from a modern perspective his errors are quickly apparent: emphasis on time-consuming walking and calisthenics lacked sufficient stimulation; omission of purposeful road training; and excessive emphasis on sprinting and interval training. Pihkala used to quote W. G. George's remark: "It's not distance but speed that kills." Yet he never made the mental connection that would have led him to see the value of extensive endurance running. He preached that short, fast exercise with proper rest intervals, if not carried to excess, will improve endurance and strength better than long, slow exercise. Pihkala's track work was too intense and his winter training too insipid. But his cross-country training was right on the mark: "Cross-country training must be an occasion for sweat but not for shortness of breath," he said.

During these early years marathon training was at a much more advanced level in Japan. Still, the Japanese had no success in the 1924 and 1928 Olympics because there were too many deviations from the current hundred miles-a-week standard, into frequent race-paced running and year-round gymnastics. The Japanese were probably handicapped in the 1920s by climatic and dietary factors as well, not to mention the long ocean voyages to the Games. But they blamed their failures on improper training philosophy and went back to the European methods, effectively eliminating themselves from the victory stand until Kitei Son's gold medal in 1936.

When Kitei Son, now a wealthy mill-owner in his native Korea, ran at Berlin in 1936, the world centered its attention to his running shoes—which were split between the big toe and the other toes—but ignored his heavy training mileage. Kitei later revealed that the shoes had been designed on a whim. His marathon time for the difficult Grunewald course must be rated equal to Emil Zatopek's Olympic record at Helsinki sixteen years later, even though the Czech's time was six minutes faster.

TABLE 2

Olympic Marathon Winners

1896	Spiridon Louis (Greece)	2:58:50.0	40.000 km.
1900	Michel Theato (France)	2:59:45.0	40.260 km.
1904	Thomas Hicks (USA)	3:28:53.0	40.000 km.
1908	John Hayes (USA)	2:55:18.4	42.195 km.
1912	Kenneth McArthur (S. Africa)	2:36:54.8	40.200 km.
1920	Hannes Kolemainen (Finland)	2:32:35.8	42.750 km.
1924	Albin Stenroos (Finland)	2:41:22.6	42.195 km.
1928	Mohammed El Ouafi (France)	2:32:57.0	42.194 km.
1932	Juan Carlos Zabala (Argentina)	2:31:36.0	42.194 km.
1936	Kitei Son (Japan/Korea)	2:29:18.2	42.194 km.
1948	Delfo Cabrera (Argentina)	2:34:51.6	42.194 km.
1952	Emil Zatopek (Czech.)	2:23:03.2	42.194 km.
1956	Alain Mimoun (France)	2:25:00.0	42.194 km.
1960	Abebe Bikila (Ethiopia)	2:15:16.2	42.194 km.
1964	Abebe Bikila (Ethiopia)	2:12:11.2	42.194 km.
1968	Mamo Wolde (Ethiopia)	2:20:26.4	42.194 km.
1972	Frank Shorter (USA)	2:12:19.8	42.194 km.
1976	Waldemar Cierpinski (E. Ger.)	2:09:55.0	42.194 km.

After World War II, training methods bore the stamp of English and Russian runners. The British runners rose to the top in European international racing largely because of two factors. First was that the mild English sea weather favored year-round training, which by this time was indispensable for the international competitor. Lacking the sharp seasonal weather changes of northern and eastern Europe, the British runners developed continuous year-round training programs. They were also the first to omit a winter break in favor of a cross-country season. The second critical factor was that the British overcame the widespread fear of running on roads. They did a majority of their training on asphalt, where the going is faster than in the woods. The Road Runners Club of England, which now has 2,400 members, provided high standards of competition and good racing conditions. Five of the eleven European marathon champions selected to date have been British (1950, 1962, 1966, 1969, and 1974). Finland follows with four (three titles before World War II), and Belgium has won once.

Following Popov Proves Fatal

The Soviet Union, having led the way in sports science for years, turned with great zeal to the theory and practice of the marathon. But marathoning never gave them successes like those of Vladimir Kuts and Piotr Bolotnikov at the shorter distances. The collective efforts of the Soviet runners were a failure, and scientific training theory had only limited influence.

The best Soviet marathon runner was Serge Popov, who won the 1958 European Championship race at Stockholm in the world-record time of 2:15:17.0. Popov's win actually set back the Soviet's training. Popov, like Kuts, used interval training, which was thought to be the secret of his success. Popov ran as many as forty repeats of 400 meters in 66-68 seconds, jogging only 60 meters in between. Though he did endurance runs of 1½ to 2½ hours between interval training days, intervals so dominated his training that he averaged only ten miles a day even on rest days. A typical week's interval work looked something like this:

Day 1   5 x 400 meters in 65-66 seconds, 15 x 1,000 meters in 2:48-2:50, 5 x 400 meters in 63-65 seconds

Day 2   40 x 400 meters in 66-68 seconds

Day 3   2 x 1,000 meters in 2:43-2:52, 3 x 2,000 meters in 5:53-5:58, 2 x 3,000 meters in 8:43-8:52, 2 x 1,000 meters in 2:55-3:00

Popov's training was much-imitated, and his interval work-outs were frequently expanded to extravagant levels. Some German runners were doing 100 x 400 meters on the track in 70 to 75 seconds. They became closely acquainted with every pebble and blade of grass in the stadium, but were overstressed and frequently ran poor races. They knew almost nothing about even pacing because they had scarcely trained for it. Yet scientific interval training—"Freiburg training," as Woldemar Gerschler referred to it—drew both young and experienced runners.

Many interval-trained runners had good race times in the spring, and then watched their times get increasingly faster. What good are a series of 65-second quarters to a marathoner?

True, his heart volume will increase and resting pulse rate will fall, but muscles become overacidified. Such runners acquire local muscle endurance only during the long runs on recovery days between interval sessions. They are running so fast most of the time that the muscles never adapt to race pace at all.

The plague of interval training spead so widely that in 1960 "natural" runners, unspoiled by intervals, completely demolished Europe's elite. These included Abebe Bikila and Morocco's Mohammed Rhadi.

The Era of Zatopek

The man who invented interval training, Emil Zatopek, had something else in mind. Zatopek, one of the great individuals of sports history, was self-coached, and combined unbounded enthusiasm with a sense of humor and earthy cleverness. The thing he lacked was great talent. But he made up for his physical deficiency by sheer energy and will, and by devising an entirely new training system. The "Czech locomotive" rolled up Olympic golds in 1948 and in 1952, winning an unprecedented triple at Helsinki in the 5,000 and 10,000 meters, as well as the marathon.

Zatopek dominated his era. Because of his uneconomical arm movements and facial contortions, people erroneously concluded that style no longer mattered in the long distances. Physical condition became the holy grail. Zatopek says he was always conscious of his own poor style, but felt he'd go farther on two years of conditioning than by wasting time tinkering around with his leg and arm movements. The runner who would beat Zatopek had to have more talent, a better running style, and at least the same training.

Zatopek's rivals in the Soviet Union, and Gerschler in Freiburg, Germany, said that intervals should be run faster, with shorter rest breaks, that the intervals should be shortened to 200 instead of 400 meters. This unnatural training method proved to be a complete mistake.

A typical day of training for Emil Zatopek included:

5 x 200 meters in 30-35 seconds
15 x 400 meters in 80-90 seconds
15 x 400 meters in 70 seconds
10 x 400 meters in 80-90 seconds
5 x 200 meters under 30 seconds

This workout provided the comprehensive training that helped Zatopek acquire his form for racing at all distances. His slow 80 to 90-second 400s, separated by rest pauses, had nearly the same effect as continuous endurance running. He interspersed long intervals with faster runs, but these were never as fast as those of his imitators. This is how Zatopek trained during his best years, 1952-53, after having previously experimented with faster intervals. When Zatopek began sprinkling his training with runs of 400 meters in 90 to 120 seconds, he broke his own world records at 5,000 and 10,000 meters in 1954, and was surprised to have done so. Zatopek said it was the quantity, not the speed, of his training that accounted for his success in the marathon in 1952 and his world records in the hour run and at 20 kilometers.

Zatopek had other tricks in his training bag, including hill running, running in heavy boots, and jumping. Running in boots strengthened and toughened him. A lot of what was written about Zatopek during his glory days was false, simply because he was an incorrigible scamp who loved to lead journalists, observers, and opponents around by the nose. He may have actually led his followers down some false paths because of this. But he complained of not being able to retain his form as long as his rival Alain Mimoun. Perhaps this was the price he paid for being a pioneer, an experimenter, and his own coach.

In later years, Europe lost their hold on the middle and long distances. This became clear at the 1960 Olympic Games in Rome, where Peter Snell, trained by Arthur Lydiard of New Zealand, won the 800 meters. Herb Elliott, coached by Australia's Percy Cerutty, won the 1,500, and another Lydiard runner, Murray Halber, won the 5,000. Of course, Abebe Bikila won the marathon. The only Olympic gold medalist in 1960 who was interval-trained was Piotr Bolotnikov of the Soviet Union, who won the 10,000 meters.

We'll discuss Arthur Lydiard's thoughts on training later on. Percy Wells Cerutty, the running coach and life-style teacher of Portsea, Australia, is among the great distance running coaches, and long ago had his middle-distance runners doing 100 miles a week. He did not, however, express any notable thoughts specific to the marathon.

How Bikila Trained

Bikila was one of the most gifted runners to race the 26-mile 385-yard distance. At 5'9" 121 pounds, he had the ideal build for a marathoner. He lived at high altitude and was the first to demonstrate its effects on long-distance performance. He trained by doing long runs over mountainous terrain, or ran more than 18 miles on the roads. Cross-country runs, including altitude variations of 2,500 feet, were part of his program. Oni Niskanen of Finland, who discovered Bikila in the Ethiopian Imperial Guard and became his coach, assigned him 1,500-meter runs as well. Bikila would run 4 x 1,500 meters around a lake, at an altitude of 5,500 feet, in 4:12-4:18, with a five-minute pause.

Although he seemed invincible, he was to know the shadowy side of life. He was favored for a third straight win in the high-altitude marathon at Mexico City in 1968, but was forced to drop out at 10½ miles with a knee injury. Then came the car crash in 1969, which put the gifted runner in a wheelchair for the remaining four years of his life. He died in October 1973.

Training for the Masses

Until the late 1950s, the marathon was strictly an event for the top runners. Then Arthur Lydiard and Dr. Ernst van Aaken helped make marathon training accessible to the masses. The two great coaches were in agreement on many essential training points. They each advocated long road runs, rejected interval training, and made specific use of race-paced running. Both of them shocked the world of traditional medicine by making marathoners out of former cardiac patients and by advocating athletics for people over forty.

Among van Aaken's proteges there was only one Olympic medalist, Harald Norpoth, silver medalist in the 5,000 meters at Tokyo in 1964. But he has indirectly guided numerous runners through his own coaching, his sports-medicine practice, and his articles and books.

While van Aaken's greatest contribution was through his public predictions and training theories, Arthur Lydiard has emerged as the great systematizer. Lydiard has been the coach of the coaches, spreading his influence by traveling around the world giving lectures and workshops, and by working for extended periods with national teams of various nations. To a large extent, Lydiard is reponsible for the resurgence of the Finnish runners during the 1970s. While Lydiard's training system can be applied word-for-word, van Aaken's system requires understanding the man's philosophy. Van Aaken presents the basics in a simple way which makes his ideas attractive to everyone. His Waldniel endurance training method is gaining increasing acceptance around the world.

Training for Oxygen Uptake

A quick look at the differences between interval training and the Waldniel endurance theory is most revealing. Freiburg interval training involves fast oxygen-debt running. Van Aaken suggests that the runner train slowly to increase his oxygen uptake. A marathoner will never enter oxygen debt while training by the Waldniel method, but will run at a steady pulse rate of 120 to 130 per minute and an average lactic acid concentration of 15 mg./percent. Intervals increase the pulse to 140-200 per minute. Van Aaken, on the other hand, recommends 80-140. Van Aaken would keep the ratio of fast training miles to endurance miles at 1:20. Van Aaken thinks that every middle- and long-distance runner has an optimal training pace and mileage depending on his particular racing event. For a pulse rate of 120, the average daily training mileages for specific racing distances are as follows:

Racing Distance	Ratio of Racing to Training Distance	Average Daily Training Distance
400 m.	1:15	3.75 miles
800 m.	1.12	6 miles
1,500 m.	1:10	10 miles
3,000 m.	1:7	12.5 miles
5,000 m.	1:5	15.5 miles
10,000 m.	1:3	18.5 miles
Marathon	1:1	26.2 miles
Ultramarathon	1:2 (after 6-8 years of training)	50 miles

According to van Aaken, "If you want to race 26 miles, you'll have to run 26 miles quite often in training." He encourages runners to go beyond the marathon distance once a week on runs as long as 50 miles. He advises marathon specialists to run 100-mile events, and predicts that runners of the future will run the marathon in 1:55 if male, 2:20 if female. To accomplish this he will have to run 50 miles in training regularly, and will have to weave other sports like bicycling into his training regimen.*

Van Aaken says that an 800-meter specialist who wants to run 1:40 or faster will have to train like a marathoner and also be able to run 400 meters in under 46 seconds. For the runner of the future, van Aaken calculates a so-called OSC Index, the formula for which is: heart volume in cubic centimeters divided by body weight in kilograms; multiplied by leg length in decimeters (10-centimeter units); then multiplied by maximal oxygen uptake in liters; and the whole thing is divided by resting pulse.

$$\frac{\text{(HV/kg. x max. } O_2 \text{ x leg length}}{\text{pulse/min.}}$$

The OSC Index for 5,000-meter silver-medalist Harald Norpoth is:

$$\frac{(1{,}243/60) \text{ x } 5.0 \text{ x } 9.5}{22} \qquad 22.2$$

For the runner of the future:

$$\frac{(1{,}250/60) \text{ x } 6.0 \text{ x } 9.7}{40} \qquad 30.2$$

Training by the van Aaken method involves a continuous expansion of one's endurance limits. This is why van Aaken is reluctant to give fixed speeds and mileages for training. However, he requests that all the runners he is coaching run at least one hour a day at endurance pace.

---

* To avoid confusion, I want to point out my personal differences of opinion here. It seems more important to me to train for the *time* you'll be on the road rather than for the *distance*. A 2:20 runner, for example, should run 2:20 quite often, and not 26 miles. Van Aaken may have his theory correct, but in practice perhaps only the runner of the future will be able to run such long distances regularly from an orthopedic point of view.

Marathon training à la van Aaken involves two fundamental tempo-training variations for the marathon specialist:

1. 1,000-meter runs at marathon race pace, repeated 20-42 times; or 1,000 meters at 10,000-meter race pace, repeated 5 to 10 times with long walking breaks

2. 2,000-3,000 meters at 1:30-2:00 minutes slower than personal best time, repeated 5 to 10 times and followed by acceleration sprints of 60-80 meters

A kind of tempo training is also included in van Aaken's "crescendo runs" for long distances. This involves continually increasing the pace and accelerating over the last third of the distance. This is specific preparation for the long accelerations required in track racing, or for an attempt at a faster second half in the marathon.

Dr. van Aaken emphasizes weight loss to 20 percent under the so-called norm and recommends occasional days of complete fasting. He says it's best to run with a slight feeling of hunger. He rejects weight training and gymnastics, in accordance with his axiom that "a person learns to run by running." Since van Aaken does not subdivide his training into yearly seasons, this makes his system agreeable to the noncompetitor. He is not a believer in cross-country and hill running, perhaps because he lives on the flat terrain of the Lower-Rhein region of Germany.

Lydiard the Organizer

Arthur Lydiard lives in mountainous New Zealand. He has concocted a unique training system that he put into practice on the lakes, forest, and volcanoes, the dominant topographical features of the area. Lydiard has tested all his theories by organizing marathon runs in which he then ran alongside his proteges.

The story is told of a marathon in which Olympic gold medalists Murray Halberg and Peter Snell were running at the front, while Snell's father and Lydiard were trotting along farther back in the field. "Anybody can run 22 miles," Lydiard says. The fact that he specifically says 22 and not 26 miles, 385 yards, shows his good understanding of the matter. The really critical problems in oxygen metabolism don't begin until after the twenty-first mile. As a result, 22 miles is the standard distance for the Sunday outings in which Lydiard's runners take part, whether middle-distance specialists or marathoners. In the early 1960s this was considered shockingly long, but today it has become a fact of life in a marathoner's training.

Lydiard's training system is ingenious. The winter season begins in April in the Southern Hemisphere (equivalent to November in North America), with sixteen weeks of cross-country training. This is followed by eight weeks of road training, ten weeks of marathon training, six weeks of hill training, and twelve weeks of track training.

The sixteen-week cross-country phase begins with races of three to six miles, later increasing to ten miles. All training runs are done on varied terrain (paths, roads, open fields). The twenty-two-mile "Lydiard long jog" is never omitted, even if it falls on the day after a cross-country race. But this difficult training regimen is preceded by several weeks of conditioning with no racing. During the first sixteen weeks of cross-country training the runner puts in 800 miles, or about forty miles a week. Lydiard alternates days of easy running with days of faster work.

During the road training phase weekly mileage rises to about seventy. The first week's schedule is something like this:

Monday	3 miles of 50-meter sprints with a jog between sprints
Tuesday	3-mile time trial
Wednesday	2 x 800 meters at 50 percent effort
Thursday	6 x 400 meters at 25 percent effort
Friday	6 x 200 meters at 50 percent effort
Saturday	one mile, very fast
Sunday	long jog, 22 miles

Lydiard recommends that all running is done on roads. During the marathon-training period—a high-mileage phase for runners of all specialties—runners average one hundred miles a week. Runners alternate runs at endurance pace over hilly terrain for ten to fifteen miles with fartlek runs over comparable distances. On Friday there is a ten-mile run at 75 percent effort, followed by a run of twenty to twenty-six miles at a relatively slow pace.

During the six-week hill-training phase there are daily runs of twelve miles. These are done on a hilly two-mile loop, with rolling hills in the first section, then a flat stretch, a steep part, and then another flat section. A relaxed springing style is practiced on the main climb, which is taxing, but is not run anaerobically. The downhill phase necessitates a long, easy stride, while the uphill section builds muscles and strengthens the legs. Lydiard swears by this aspect of his training system. According to him, it is the fastest way of getting in condition for the racing season.

The three months of track training are even more varied. Quarter-effort intervals of 20 x 200 meters (given a best time of 26 seconds, they would be run in 35 seconds) are alternated with runs of fifteen to eighteen miles at 25 percent effort (about five or six minutes slower than best time). There is a 3 x 200 meters all-out effort on Friday, a regular twenty-two to twenty-eight-mile run on Saturday, a normal run of fifteen miles on Sunday.

I feel that this last phase is too inflexible, and not as convincing as the rest of Lydiard's system. The training of world-class runners tends to be broken down into a larger number of workouts, so that training is geared more specifically to the needs of the individual runner. Not everyone can apply this phase of the Lydiard system; veteran runners, for example, should not attempt to do 3 x 200 meters all-out and then come back the next day for a twenty-eight-mile run.

It's interesting that Lydiard, whose main strength is preparing runners for long track events, has his runners jog only three to six miles on the last three days before a championship race. On the Monday before a Saturday race he has them do 3 x 200 meters at 75 percent effort and then on Tuesday, a mile run at 75 percent effort. The mixture of training methods is important. The marathon runner must be more flexible in his training than a 400-meter runner, because road running is hard muscle work that requires varied workouts, especially as one enters the faster racing categories.

Van Aaken, an exponent of long endurance running, warned against running too many miles. He felt the total should never exceed 500 to 600 miles a month, including occasional longer runs up to fifty miles. Gaston Roelants and Jos Hermens, for example, ran up to thirty miles a day in preparation for Montreal and lived to regret it.

Presumably, the wise old men of training will soon be replaced by running collectives and running teams. Already, Wildor Hollmann, at the Sports Institute of the University of Cologne in Germany, has determined the endurance limits of long-distance runners. Now the coach presumably needs only to arrange training schedules for his athletes in accordance with the appropriate guidelines. Hollmann's discoveries at Cologne are also being duplicated at East Germany's University of Physical Culture in Leipzig.

Chapter 6

Marathoning for Over Forty

Since 1960, the marathon has had an increasingly strong attraction for men and women in the second half of life. Veteran runners have popularized the sport to the point where nearly everyone can compete successfully within his own age-group. For the age-group runner, finishing is far more important than placing.

Former world-class athletes who have competed in other disciplines are now running the marathon. The former 400-meter hurdles champion from Germany, Wolfgang Fischer, runs a three-hour marathon at age forty-five. Bank president Friedrich Tempel began running at sixty-five, improving to a 3:15:54 marathon at age seventy. Seventy-nine-year-old Arthur Lambert ran a 3:52:50 marathon, and Christos Iordanides of Greece ran it in 6:42 at age ninety-six. Though these are unbelievable performances for older men, even runners in younger age-groups are astonishing medical authorities with their race times. Jack Foster of New Zealand, for example, who began running at age thirty-two, ran a 20-mile world record at age thirty-nine and represented his country in the Olympic marathon. At forty-one, he ran 2:11:18 to finish second at the Christchurch Commonwealth Games. At forty-four, he again ran the Olympic marathon, and at nearly forty-five ran in the world cross-country championships at Dusseldorf, placing thirty-third, ahead of three world record-holders.

Jack Foster's experience confirms the belief that a runner can hold his marathon times at par until at least the age of forty. Foster did not have the advantage of taking a year off from studies and work to devote himself exclusively to running, as younger world-class runners often do. He has a family to support, and, as a result, has missed a number of big races because of his limited free time.

Algerian-born Alain Mimoun of France has run his whole life. He was a silver medalist at the 1948 and 1952 Olympics in the 10,000 meters, running second to Zatopek in 1948 and 1952. At thirty-five, he ran a 2:25 in Melbourne to win the marathon at the 1956 Games, beating the great Zatopek. Mimoun, who never retired, now runs mostly half-marathons. In 1968 he ran a 30:47 10,000 meters, which bettered his silver medal time in 1948. Mimoun has also been able to maintain his marathon performances for twenty years. In 1975 he won the French veterans' half-marathon championship at age fifty-four, in a time that makes me think he could still run the full 26 miles in under 2:25.

Sweden's Erik Ostbye has drunk from a different fountain of youth. He eats mainly raw foods, and does all his training in forest and field, and does not worry if paths are unavailable. His running history is astonishing: at forty he ran 2:18 on a short course; at forty-four, 2:23:05; at forty-six, 2:20:12; at forty-seven, 2:20:45; at forty eight, 2:23:56; at forty-nine, 2:24:34; and at fifty, 2:28:48. This last time was probably the result of an off-year for Erik, since he came back at age fifty-one to record a 2:25:19. At fifty-three, Ostbye ran 2:33 and at fifty-four, 2:29.

Track & Field News publishes yearly tables of world age-group records for runners from early childhood to advanced age. The tables show that performance losses in the marathon through age are the least of any event. A sprinter slows down at age twenty-five; a jumper is past his prime at thirty. Ignoring the rare exceptions, like four-time Olympic discus gold medalist Al Oerter, athletes over thirty-five have little chance of Olympic success except in the marathon or the 50-kilometer walk.

The performance curve of a marathon runner drops in a slow, parabolic curve. Here is table showing performance for runners over twenty-five years of age.

TABLE 3

Percentage of Full Performance for Long-Distance Races

Age	5,000 m.	10,000 m.	Marathon
25	100%	100%	99%
30	100%	100%	100%
35	97%	98%	99%
40	93%	94%	96%
45	88%	90%	92%
50	83%	85%	88%
55	77%	79%	82%
60	70%	73%	76%
65	64%	66%	70%
70	56%	59%	63%
75	49%	51%	55%

The Pulse of Potential

Why the marathon boom? Sports medicine has some interesting answers. After age forty, individuals can no longer demand extremely fast movement from their muscles, tendons, joints, and ligaments. In addition, skeletal bones lose flexibility with age. But maximal oxygen uptake tapers off gradually, so people in advanced age can still process six to eight times as much oxygen while exercising as at rest. If they remain runners, their resting pulse rates will remain slow, while blood pressure rises only minimally.

To determine the most favorable endurance exercise pace, use the following formula: 180 less the runner's age in years. This corresponds to a moderate marathon training pace, with pulse rates of 120-40. According to Dr. van Aaken, a working pulse of 130 per minute is the ideal rate.

Other factors point toward doing extreme endurance running after age forty. Changes in metabolism beyond the thirtieth year result in a lower internal caloric demand. So if a person exercises little, his body weight will rise. Men get the oft-caricatured paunch, while women tend to gain weight in the hips and upper thighs. However, older marathon runners of both sexes find their weight naturally stabilizing at healthy levels.

The active marathon runner gets a high degree of protection against "diseases of civilization," such as coronary infarctions, diabetes, and arteriosclerosis. Marathon runners can expect to *enjoy* their advancing years—quite aside from health protection—and will probably extend their life expectancy by several years. Dr. van Aaken's tests on elderly runners indicated that endurance running may offer a certain measure of protection against cancer.

Dr. Thomas Bassler, a marathoner and physician, after conducting tests on hundreds of marathon runners, spoke of "immunization" against heart attack. Bassler suggests that immunization begins when a person has run 1,000 miles. This means that six months of running forty-eight-miles weeks offers protection against coronary infarction and angina pectoris. Both van Aaken's and Bassler's ideas are controversial because they don't yet have statistical support. But their critics make things a little too easy for themselves, demanding proof without supplying counter-evidence.

While a person's life-span is not fixed, let us assume that the total number of heartbeats in a lifetime are 2.57 billion for seventy years—our current average life expectancy. Marathon runners who train from age forty until the end of their years will have heart rates of about 50, rather than 70, beats per minute throughout those years, thereby lightening his heart's workload. For a total of 2.57 billion heartbeats, such individuals could theoretically live to age eighty-two. My bold theory is that they will. And if they been running their whole lives, their average resting heart rates would take them to the ripe old age of ninety-eight. Even though their heart rates may rise to 130 while training, and even higher in races, marathon runners still gain many years through significant overall economy.

Living habits tend to change when one trains for the marathon. Older runners naturally stop smoking and cut back on drinking. They avoid unhealthy foods and overeating, do not take drugs, and enjoy deep, refreshing sleep because of the positive effects of running on the sympathetic nervous system. They tend to treat their heart and lungs with the care that other men lavish on their automobiles; as a result, they suffer fewer crashes. They'll take vacations that allow for lots of running instead of passively lying in the sun for hours. In this way, running marathons can change a person's entire life-style. Running may even lead a person into sociopolitical action against pollution; nuclear power plants; and the replacement of priceless open, agricultural lands by freeways and housing tracts.

The man or woman who runs marathons for decades on end is far less vulnerable to the stresses of civilized living—especially if he avoids bitterly competitive attitudes and faces new challenges with the wisdom appropriate to his years. He should avoid the obsessive attitude of the adolescent competitor.

Even if one is over forty, there need be no significant changes in training. The runner over forty, male or female, can follow the same training plans as younger runners, simply adjusting them to slower time categories. Depending on one's temperamental inclinations, the older runner can make certain variations:

- Do fewer tempo runs.
- Occasionally, do an extremely long run of several hours at a slow pace.
- Occasionally enter ultramarathon races.
- Pay more attention to even pace while racing.

The older marathoner, if well trained, is less vulnerable to heat than the young runner. This is clearly revealed by the dropout statistics for the different age-groups. The older runner's well-tuned metabolism reacts less drastically to heat stresses. Symptoms of running for decades on the roads, such as sciatica, may actually be ameliorated by the heat. In cold weather, the older runner is more susceptible to muscle cramping. Thus, he should dress warmly and massage his hands with a heating liniment. Older runners get colder because of decreased capillarization of the small ciliary blood vessels.

Chapter 7

Women and Marathoning

The first marathon only for women was held in 1973 at Waldniel, Germany. But the first notable attempts by women to run the marathon were as unofficial entrants in men's races. At the 1967 Boston Marathon, Kathy Switzer, disguised in heavy clothing, was physically manhandled by an organizer who attempted to remove her from the course, even though she finished the race. The three-hour barrier was first broken by a woman in 1971, when Beth Bonner ran it in 2:55:22. Six years later, when Chantal Langlace of France held the world women's record with 2:33:15, there were already an estimated one thousand women marathon runners worldwide. At the 1977 Boston race alone, there were 140 women entrants. The present rate of increase will most likely continue, and it's safe to predict that eventually there will be as many women as men marathoning, at least in the industrialized countries.

To say it up front: no woman will ever run faster than the men's world record. Basic speed and muscle strength play too great a role in the marathon, though they are relatively unimportant in the extreme long distances. Californian Natalie Cullimore, for example, won a 100-mile race in 16:11, ahead of all the male entrants. And women have continually stolen channel-swimming records away from men.

One thing is undeniable. As Dr. van Aaken claimed over twenty years ago, women are better adapted by nature for running the long distances than men, both physically and psychologically. Ludwig Prokop, president of the world organization of sports physicians, and Dr. Josef Nocker have reaffirmed in a recent book that the female is the weaker sex. However, their concepts are outdated. Men are predestined to excel at sprinting, jumping, and throwing because of their superior biomechanical gifts; but women have the advantage in biochemical terms. It's not enough to bring women on par with men at world-class racing levels, but this does open doors for women in the essentially metabolic discipline of marathoning. Childbirth is easily the greatest human metabolic endurance performance. Females are specially adapted to handle this, as well as other extreme metabolic changes.

A few of the classic physical differences between men and women are:

	Man	Woman
Average ideal weight	154 lbs.	121 lbs.
% water by body weight	60%	52%
% muscle by body weight	40%	23%

Lighter weight gives women a clear advantage. Most world-class women marathoners weigh under 120 pounds (Miki Gorman weighs 88 and Lydia Ritter weighs 92), which allows them to forget about weight gain during the marathon. Instead of burning 2,600 calories or more during a race, the woman runner will need only 2,100 or less. Her glycogen reserves are the same as that of a man, giving her the ability to run 26 miles without consuming any additional nutrients. The percentage of fat in a woman's body varies enormously, but in all cases it is higher than a man's.

Active body fat serves as a great storehouse for energy metabolism, compared with the "small change" of glycogen. On average, a woman has 25 percent fat content by body weight. In older, inactive women the figure may rise to 30 percent, with the typical appearance of fatty deposits on hips and upper thighs (the female parallel to the male paunch).

Dr. Joan Ullyot, a world-class marathoner, and medical researcher with two 2:58 times, measured a 17 percent fat content for her own body. Dr. Ullyot began running to lose weight, as did another world-class competitor, Manuela Angenvoorth. Dr. Ullyot retained the advantages of relatively high body fat even after having slimmed down as she desired. She says that a well-trained woman will always have 10 percent more body fat than an equally well trained man.

TABLE 4

Women's World Marathon Records (1967-77)

1967	Maureen Wilton (Canada)	3:15:22
1967	Anni Peede (W. Germany)	3:07:26
1970	Caroline Walker (USA)	3:02:53
1971	Beth Bonner (USA)	3:01:42
1971	Sarah Berman (USA)	3:00:35
1971	Beth Bonner (USA)	2:55:22
1971	Cheryl Bridges (USA)	2:49:40
1973	Miki Gorman (USA)	2:46:36
1974	Chantal Langlace (France)	2:46:24
1974	Jackie Hansen (USA)	2:43:54
1975	Liane Winter (W. Germany)	2:42:24
1975	Christa Vahlensieck (W. Germany)	2:40:15
1975	Jackie Hansen (USA)	2:38:19
1977	Chantal Langlace (France)	2:35:15
1977	Christa Vahlensieck (W. Germany)	2:34:47

Dr. van Aaken cites further advantages for the woman runner. Women's lower body water content (52 percent compared with men's 60 percent) improves the availability of metabolic substances. Since women have the sex hormone estrogen, more of their body water is stored in the connective tissue than that of men. Thus, body water is more readily available for endurance work. Van Aaken says a woman's adrenal cortex is 10 percent larger than a man's, and its production of hormones is correspondingly greater.

Women's enzyme systems seem better able to metabolize fats. Further, women have more available sulfur. These reasons account for women's ability to adapt to long distances relatively quickly, without years of preparation, as well as for their ability to handle the long distances with less trauma than men.

Iron: The Debate over a Deficiency

After all these advantages women runners have, one might imagine there would be no limit to the possible performances of women. But women also have some disadvantages. The most striking of these is that hemoglobin levels can fall rapidly when a woman runs long distances. Although this phenomenon sometimes occurs in men as well, statistics show that women—perhaps because of menstrual losses—have a lower hemoglobin content than men.

There's a raging battle among the experts over the best way to treat low hemoglobin levels. Dr. Ullyot tells her running companions to take regular iron supplements. English physician and marathoner Dr. John Brotherhood warns that iron supplementation has toxic effects when continued over long periods. He considers low hemoglobin a false symptom, since the runner's total blood volume increases faster than her red blood corpuscles. Thus, he warns both men and women against pills. Dr. van Aaken, who has probably examined more female marathon runners than anyone else, also minimizes the significance of iron-deficiency symptoms. He credits women with a greater iron-binding capacity, which allows them to get along on less hemoglobin. Research on leading women marathoners by Dr. Jung of Munster, Germany led to confusing results: runners with the lowest hemoglobin values were the fastest. He, too, interprets low hemoglobin as a false deficiency. On the other hand, sudden losses of form in female distance runners occur in connection with lowered iron content in the body. Strictly on the basis of experience, I advised Christa Vahlensieck years ago to take iron pills at the noon meal on the days before menstruation as a preventive measure. Since it does no harm, I'll stick to this preventive treatment, because it obviously does no harm. If pills and occasional sour vomiting are not tolerable, the runner can buy iron-rich mineral water or she can simply eat steamed spinach or lightly cooked calf's liver.

The menstrual period has already been mentioned as a background factor. For many women, blood losses are an obstacle to running. But women soon find that, not only does running have negative effects during menstruation, it actually tends to alleviate cramps and headaches. No female athletes in any sport report negative effects from exercise during the menstrual period. Some female runners actually feel a positive effect, though this was almost certainly a psychological phenomenon, due to the emotional ups and downs that many women experience prior to the onset of the period. Christa Vahlensieck beat the women's world marathon elite in 1976 on the first day of an early period. It is by no means rare for a woman's period to start early in the excitement of a race. Manipulations to postpone the period, like taking birth-control pills longer than the prescribed time, are not advisable. The body seeks its own means of relieving stress, and if it isn't allowed to function through the normal channels will seek other, abnormal ones.

Should a woman run during pregnancy? Dr. Joan Ullyot says yes. The amniotic fluid protects the baby like a fish in an aquarium. Training can continue, but racing and interval workouts should be avoided in favor of long, slow distance. Miki Gorman's experience showed that running through a pregnancy doesn't interfere with the birth of a healthy child and that a quick return to form is possible afterward. Miki became pregnant at about the time of her 1974 Boston victory, and then 11 months later, after the birth of her first child (by a Caesarean), ran a personal best time, at age forty-one, of 2:39:11—the second fastest ever for a woman at the time.

The rumor frequently circulates that running causes a woman's breasts to become pendulous. This, too, can be dismissed as fiction. Dr. Ullyot says in her book *Women's Running* that pendulous breasts are caused by the inner structure of the breast muscles, especially when there is ample fat structure, and not by running. This fat decreases through running, which eventually makes the breasts smaller and firmer.

It is untrue that women in sports age more quickly than nonrunners. To begin with, women live an average of three years longer than men. And in any case it's not logical that women would lose vitality sooner by adopting a more active life-style. This misconception may stem from the mental image of the average forty-year-old matron of a former day. The vitality of older women marathoners is indicated by comparing two world age-group records for women: eleven-year-old Mary Etta Boitano's 3:01 and forty-five-year-old Ursula Blaschke's 2:56:12.5.

Sports medicine has been of the opinion until recently that a woman's heart volume cannot be increased to the same extent as a man's through training. But Dr. van Aaken showed that a number of good women runners, for example Anni Pede, have hearts with volumes of 1,000 cc. Christa Vahlensieck's heart volume was measured at 992 cc. which, when compared to her body weight, is nearly the peak value obtainable by men.

Down with High Heels

For many years, fashion prescribed a high-heeled shoe for women, to increase their height, to make their legs look longer and thinner, and to give her a tripping gait suggestive of delicacy and fragility. In this age of clogs and other low-heeled shoes, though, high heels will hopefully become an anachronism. Unfortunately, women have a hard time getting down off their dress shoes. In fact, those shoes may represent the single most difficult step into distance running for women. High heels shorten the Achilles tendon, creating serious foot problems when women take up distance running, especially on the roads. Regardless of any other good running characteristics the woman may have, the switch to running shoes can cause problems as serious as stress fractures, which strangely are more common in women than men, despite lower body weight. The foot has often been additionally deformed by wearing narrow, pointed shoes.

A woman who wants to start running will have to swear off high heels from the start. Her running shoes, at least at the beginning, should have a definite heel, even if it takes home-made foam inserts to provide a comfortable lift (not rigid or solid inserts). In time the inserts can be removed. The leg and foot muscles will gain strength, first through running, and later the bones and tendons will also be strengthened. Foot exercises —like running barefoot on a carpet or for 100 yards on the grass, and bending toward a wall from 6 feet out without raising the heel—are also useful for helping the process along.

The greatest advantage for the beginning woman runner is that women have lower body weight relative to men. Women who begin running to lose weight generally wind up disappointed. After two or three months there may even be a weight gain, while a man may lose a few pounds in the same period. Many women begin running after thirty, never having done any sports earlier in their lives. At that point muscles are in a state of relative atrophy, so initially they'll build muscle tissue. Though the fatty cushions disappear, the difference is not noticeable on the scales. Later on, as muscle formation decreases, the women's figures slim down close to the desired ideal.

Running on asphalt presents fewer problems for women

because of their lower weight, especially if they can get rid of the common cross-legged running style during the first few weeks. This error of style is almost exclusive to men; men more often attack the road with a heavy, stamping gait.

Where training is concerned, there are scarcely any differences between men and women. For this reason, we can dispense with special training plans for women. Stress loads must be assumed, just as for a man, depending on basic speed and current level of conditioning. Women and men are equally trainable. Women require fewer tempo runs than men, and no extremely fast time trials. Women recover faster than men between training runs after races.

Chapter 8

The Marathon Is Child's Play

In Germany, the last skirmish in the battle for official recognition of age-group distance running was fought in the area of distance events for school-age children. In March 1977 the German track and field federation voted for complete removal of age limitations on racing distances up to the 100 kilometers. This was a complete turnaround from the former practice of bringing children along slowly to the longer events via sprints and middle-distance racing.

In America, things changed more quickly. After a few years of controversy, the Road Runner's Club of America began allowing children and adolescents to run long distances. In 1969, Mary Etta Boitano, then only six years old, ran the marathon in 4:27:32, accompanied by her parents and brother Mike. By no means did the early effort ruin Mary Etta for future sports participation. At the age of eleven she ran the marathon in a world-class time of 3:01, placing fourth in the U.S. women's championship race. She was carefully observed by Dr. Joan Ullyot, who said that Mary Etta recovered faster than her grown-up counterparts.

The fat was in the fire. For years it has been axiomatic that the longer the distance, the more dangerous it is for a child. In Germany during the 1950s, the longest distances adolescents were allowed to run were: at fourteen, 75 meters; at sixteen, 1,000 meters; at eighteen, 3,000 meters; at nineteen, 5,000 and 10,000 meters; and at twenty-one, the marathon. Once or twice a year there were 600-meter forest runs for the under-fourteen age-group, 2,000-meter runs for those under sixteen, and 3,000-meter runs for those under eighteen.

Running theory was stamped with the concepts of interval training and dominated by its main interpreter, Waldemar Gerschler. As a thirteen-year-old, I was limited to competing in a three-event "run, jump, and throw," in which the run was just seventy-five meters long. Since I was small and wiry, none of these events interested me. The seventy-five-meter run was over before I ever really got in gear. This was a frustrating repression of my nature. I would have switched to soccer, which I played passionately and for long hours between the ages of twelve and fourteen, had not accidental blinding of one eye reduced my view of play and depth perception. So, instead of becoming a left wing—the position played by my hero of the 1954 world-champion West German team, Horst Eckel—I became a marathon runner.

Slowly I worked my way up from one distance to another, and along the way was forcibly removed from races of 1,000 and 10,000 meters. At thirteen, I already thought that it would have been more appropriate to oust all those wheezing, fat-bellied runners around me. At fourteen I won the district forest-running title at 600 meters, though I almost fainted at the finish line. In my 1,000-meter races at age fifteen I felt the distance might be too long. I regularly came apart at around 600 meters. At the time, I did not understand that the runners ahead of me were not great talents, but merely a little accelerated in their growth.

It was many years later that I learned through the writings of Dr. Ernst van Aaken that the short middle distances like 600 and 1,000 meters are totally unsuitable for school children. But we were all caught up in the competitive order and spirit of the day. For decades the child's natural endurance has been ignored. Only under strong fire from those who clearly understood it have children been allowed to run distances. I've personally fought continuously for the extension of endurance runs for children and adolescents, precisely because I was forced for so long to run events far removed from my natural talents.

Since children cannot enter significant oxygen debt, it is quite proper that there are now no 400-meter races for children in Germany. Though children have great natural endurance, they do not have the muscle structure to run sprints in optimal style.

The Child and the World-Class Athlete

For years, Dr. Ernst van Aaken was a single voice crying in the wilderness, advocating endurance running for children. Most coaches had no concept of physical endurance, and measured everything in terms of horsepower, reaction speed, and absolute strength performances.

Van Aaken found that for the healthy, playful child, a significant indicator of endurance—heart volume in cubic centimeters (cc.) divided by weight in kilograms—can be similar to adult world-class athletes. The following values were measured for thirty-six children living in the vicinity of van Aaken's home town of Waldniel, Germany:

TABLE 5

Heart Quotient Values

Age	Height (meters)	Heart Volume (cc.)	Weight (kg.)	Heart Quotient
6	1.16	316	20.7	15.3
7	1.19	371	22.8	16.4
8	1.27	352	25.9	13.6
9	1.32	353	25.3	14.0
10	1.35	357	29.0	12.3
11	1.40	442	34.3	12.9
12	1.46	463	37.0	12.5

Compared with the average for 23 untrained adolescents 16 years of age:

16	1.80	540	72.0	7.5

Compared with 1960 Olympic 100-meter gold medalist Armin Hary:

23	1.82	606	71	8.5

Compared with 1964 5,000-meter silver medalist Harald Norpoth:

20	1.83	1,243	58.0	21.4

World-class middle-distance runners had heart quotients between 14 and 16 (Herbert Schade 16.9, Paul Schmidt 13.9, Herbert Misalla 14.0).

Children have certain physiological advantages in their favor:

- low weight
- relatively large heart
- favorable strength-to-weight ratio resulting from the above factors
- minimal orthopedic stresses while running on hard surfaces

The child's power-to-weight ratio is even more favorable than that of a woman. Calorie consumption is so low that the child's normal muscle glycogen is probably sufficient for running marathons. This must be what actually happens, because it is the only way to explain the complete absence of a crash point in well-trained children. Children also score peak values for Wildor Hollmann's endurance quotient—oxygen uptake at a pulse of 130 divided by body weight in kilograms.

The transition from dirt paths to hard road surfaces, so frequently traumatic for adults, is scarcely noticed by the child. Children fairly float over the pavement with their light-footed style, experiencing no added stresses if they wear decent shoes.

The pre-pubescent child's advantages as a runner are lost to some extent when he enters adolescence. Rapid gains in height deteriorate the heart quotient; body weight rises while heart volume remains relatively stable. Lever relationships also change for the worse at the onset of adolescence. Youths thirteen to sixteen temporarily loose momentum as distance runners. This makes it all the sadder that endurance running is still taboo in the schools. Running is even forbidden in some schoolyards because of the danger of accidents, while some schools actually have smoking rooms—which gives a strange perspective on values. Endurance running is not on the program at Germany's national youth games or in the "Youth Trains for Olympia" program. In Switzerland the situation is the same and in Austria it's even worse. But, in East Germany it was recognized long ago that thirteen-year-olds are ready to run 10-kilometer road races.

I have not included the world age-group records in this chapter because I feel there is a tendency to place too much emphasis on competition among young people. The frenzied search for a world nine-year-old marathon record belongs strictly to the goal structure of parents and coaches. A child is completely satisfied by the enormous task of running from point X to point Y. We should respect this childlike consciousness and give it free rein, so that the child's psychological performance reserves will be intact in the future. We should remind ourselves, though, that a ten-year-old boy or girl can perform physically on a par with a sixty-year-old veteran runner, but that the child will run the same times with less training.

This leads us to one disadvantage that children have when racing long distances: the young psyche. A child runs according to his feelings and is susceptible to moods and impressions gained during the run. A child could not comprehend this statement of a world-class runner: "All I was aware of was that the course was flat and somebody gave me my splits every five miles." The child is simply unable to subordinate his inner world of feelings to an outer abstract goal. He may feel like dashing off to one side or the other, shooting ahead, or running back the way he came. Children are seldom gifted with a sense of even pace. No ambitious coach or father can easily drive the child beyond the pain barrier. Nor should he try to do so, in the best interests of his charge. The child who is overtaxed simply stands still—he's just not in the mood anymore and sees absolutely no reason for continuing when he is this exhausted. Hopefully this natural psychological brake will be effective in dampening the consequences of external adult control.

Six to ten miles is a legitimate distance for eight- to twelve-year-olds—one they can handle in normal racing categories without loss of concentration or rhythm. In nature all things seek a balance. At these distances children can choose their own pace, as long as they're not handicapped by lack of training, poor sleep, or disease. The child instinctively starts races of these distances at an intelligent pace, in contrast to middle distances on the track.

Endurance running should become both fun and a sport to be continued for a lifetime. The child should be led as early as possible into playful one-hour endurance runs, if possible via fun-runs or school programs. Whenever childlike aspects can be brought into running, this should be done. The best one is easy-paced running in groups, with continuous conversation—the proof that oxygen metabolism is being held in aerobic balance. When a child discovers a pretty flower or rare mushroom in the woods, there's no need to push him on to finish the training run. Let him increase his capacity for observation and experience by running long distances with these unplanned stops. For a child under ten, running times are secondary to the experiences he is absorbing during the run.

First the Marathon, Then the Half-Mile

If parents or coaches adopt a relaxed attitude, a running program cannot possibly damage the healthy child. As the climax of a natural endurance-running experience, marathon running is a healthy accomplishment for the twelve- to fourteen-year-old. A completed marathon, regardless of finishing time, is the basis for later running activity. Organic conditioning and training the will are departure points for later specialization. I can easily imagine an age-group champion at 800 meters who will run a four-hour marathon at age twelve, later specializing in the base of his endurance-conditioning experience. The recipe of "shorter-to-longer" is not a holy of holies. Some of us will probably have to revise our thinking in this respect.

Endurance running does not make you slower. When I was entered in the German team championships to run the 1,500 meters, I neglected to train by the current schoolbook method of doing five or six 400-meter intervals the day before the event at race pace. I deliberately ran a slow nineteen miles instead, going to no trouble to imitate race pace, but trying to stay relaxed for as long as possible. On marathon training alone I ran 3:57. If I had trained running short intervals I would have had sore muscles, and probably would have run no better than 3:59. The principle here is even more valid in the case of the child. The endurance-trained youngster must be led into race-paced running by way of very low numbers of 100- or 200-meter accelerations during the course of a long run. The child's organic capacities alone will deliver him into the world of middle-distance track racing with excellent prospects.

Now we'll talk about actual mileages in training. On principle, you will have to refer to other chapters, because a six- to eighteen-year-old should train similarly to an adult, at least as far as pace is concerned. The pre-pubescent child and the adolescent with a background of endurance running have important points in their favor. Twenty-five miles a week of training is sufficient for a ten-year-old to run 3:30; an adult weighing 165 pounds would have difficulty running 4:30 on the same mileage. Favorable power-to-weight ratio and low calorie consumption with no threat of a crash point should be used before they're forever lost.

Gunther Mielke, the West German national marathon champion in 1975 and 1977, said that man has a "biochemical memory." Stated simply, this means, "You've done it before, so you can do it again." Running the marathon before adolescence will help.

The training I'll recommend for the ten- to twelve-year-old marathon runner is so simple that I'm almost embarrassed to write it: run 1 hour at an easy pace three to four times a week for a distance of about 6½ miles each time. Then once a week run two hours at the same pace. Increasing training mileage at this age may have no advantages at all, since metabolic processes are less subject to change through training in the youthful body than they are in the adult runner.

After age fourteen, training must increase in order to compensate for increased body weight relative to heart volume. Besides endurance runs, the adolescent will need occasional tempo runs and other training elements that the younger runner can ignore completely. The post-fourteen-year-old should train according to one of the groups that will be discussed in later chapters (beginner, four-hour marathon, or three-hour marathon). At that stage, he should be grateful for his favorable power-to-weight ratio.

Part Two

Getting Ready to Race

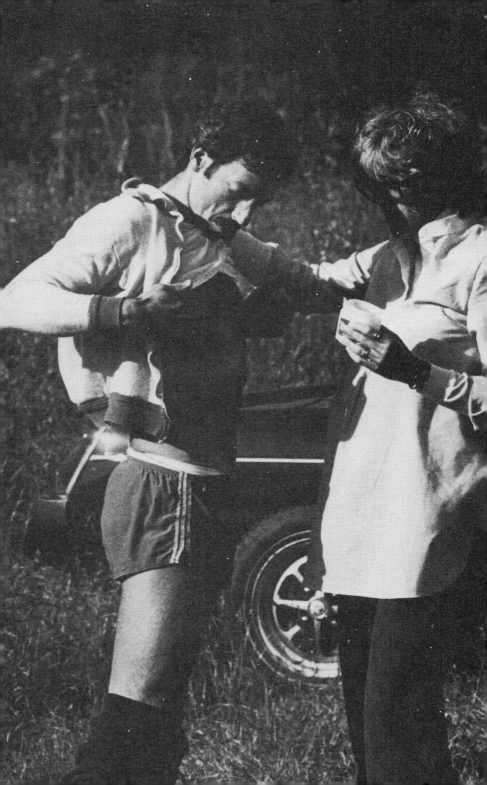

Chapter 9

Your First Marathon

A first marathon can be one of life's peak experiences: butterflies and joy all mixed up together, like high school graduation or your first driver's test. But the agonizing difference between the marathon and all your prior worldly passages is that you don't really know if you're ready. The careful student of the marathon must rely to a great extent on hearsay. There are very few marathon coaches, and those few are either busy with elite runners or refuse to share their secrets. There are few books on marathoning that contain up-to-date information. This is because until recently it was unthinkable that a man-killing event like the marathon would ever evolve into a hobby of the masses.

The One-Year Base

The first prerequisite for running the marathon is a training period of at least one year and a best time for six miles of at least fifty minutes. If you can't fill one or the other of these conditions, it would be best to delay your first adventure into the 26-mile distance. If you persist despite the warning, you'll risk winding up with a completely false impression of the marathon. Going into the race on too little base conditioning will demand a tremendous one-time effort of your body, and you will likely lose all satisfaction in the marathon for a long time—probably forever. Because of this, there is much more profit to be gained by waiting. Set your sights on the marathon only if you're in peak condition and health.

Since you can't really simulate the training marathon, don't try. Things may be going fine at eighteen miles, when suddenly it turns into a whole different ball game. Even well-conditioned Olympians have looked strong early in the race, but then faded pitifully after reaching the crash points between nineteen and twenty miles. The beginner must be extremely careful in his preparation if he expects to meet physical demands he's never encountered.

Programming Your Progress

The reason for all this negative talk isn't by any means to make you fear the marathon. On the contrary, after all the warnings have been given, we can say confidently that in no other sport will you make such rapid, sure progress with consistent training as in long-distance running. Every mile you run at a "steady-state" pace (where oxygen intake and demand are equal) constitutes measurable progress. The odds predict that a fun-runner with a best six-mile time of forty-five minutes can beat another marathon runner who's faster at six miles simply by increasing his mileage by thirty percent. Even a world-class runner will slip drastically through the ranks if he is suddenly able to train only once a week. Talent, style, and tactical knowledge count for little if the mileage isn't there. On just one workout a week, even Frank Shorter would soon be running 2:40, which can be matched by a reasonably talented runner with a best six-mile time of thirty-four minutes or by the world's best women runners.

The upper limit of effective distance training is about 125 miles per week, though a few world-class runners are able to handle mileage of 150-60 miles. For most people with limited free time, forty to sixty miles a week is plenty.

No Need for Speed

The marathoner has no need for fast tempo running. Only five percent of a runner's total mileage should be run at race pace (compared with 10 percent for a 10,000-meter specialist). In an actual marathon, the runner goes beyond aerobic pace only in the last mile or two, providing he still has sufficient circulation in his peripheral muscles to allow him to pick up the pace—a very rare thing. The marathoner's calves generally feel like rice pudding after twenty-three miles, a sure sign of either insufficient local muscle endurance (which is acquired by long endurance training runs), or of poor metabolic adaptation.

The Case for a Flat First Marathon

Find yourself a nice easy course for your first marathon—one with few uphill sections and no running on trails, which take too much out of you during the last half of the race. You can get used to running on hard surfaces by doing about half of your training on the roads for three months prior to the race. You should plan your estimated split times for the race, since the key to success is good pacing. If you start too fast, the result is disaster. If you blast off to a fast start, you may accomplish little more than cutting ten minutes off your overall race time. It is not rare in the marathon for a runner to have a full one-minute lead at twenty-four miles and then to be caught and passed before the finish. Marathoning is the art of waiting, of good nerves and concentration. Of course, these must be added to basic endurance if you're to have a successful race.

Little things sometimes make all the difference. For instance, never wear new shoes for a marathon. You should run at least fifty miles in your racing shoes before racing in them. New socks, which tend to slip around inside your shoes, can also create problems. New shoes and socks both cause blisters, one of the greatest banes of the sport. The blister that makes its first appearance at twenty miles will be smashed against the pavement several thousand times before the race ends. At that point, the only thing to do is to up muster some calm courage. But blisters can be avoided by doing sufficient training. Toes can be protected with Band-Aids (try them first on long training runs), as can nipples and any other friction-sensitive areas of the body. Try Vaseline or some other protective salve on vulnerable areas in the crotch or buttocks. You might also try salves, creams, and powders on your feet.

The 10,000-Meter Test

Let's say you have at least one full year of endurance running behind you. Your first marathon is two weeks away. At this point, you should go out and run a 10,000-meter time trial test. If your time is more than one or two minutes slower than your personal best, you should seriously consider postponing your debut in the marathon. Two minutes at 10,000 meters (or six miles) is equivalent to a loss of ten to fifteen minutes in the marathon.

If you can run a 10,000-meter personal best in a fairly secure and confident fashion, it will be a lot easier to stay on your planned marathon splits. Don't worry about falling off your planned pace and having to juggle times in your head, especially if you've chosen a good, flat and windless course. If your training, your 10,000-meter test, and your choice of course have all been optimal, you'll be able to run at a very even pace, ignoring everyone else and concentrating strictly on your planned times. (A good way to relieve yourself of the chore of memorizing splits is to write them on your arm with a ball-point pen.)

Here's a suggested training schedule for the last two weeks before your first marathon:

Day	Training
1	10,000-meter time trial no slower than 1-2 minutes under personal record, attempting a personal best time
2	easy 1-hour run
3	rest
4	easy 2-hour run
5	warmup, then 3 x 3 miles at race pace
6	20-mile run, 10 minutes slower than projected marathon pace; 20 minutes slower if projected marathon time is 4:00 or slower
7	rest
8	1½-hour aerobic run
9	6-mile run at marathon race pace
10	1½-hour easy run
11	1-hour aerobic run
12	45-minute aerobic run
13	rest
14	30-minute relaxed, enjoyable run with variations in pace
15	marathon race

The Pause that Refreshes

After your first successful marathon, take a break to let your body recover. Don't plan on running another marathon a few weeks after the first. You've bought your first race by the installment plan; now you have to make the payments. Eight weeks is the recommended interval between marathons. You can start training normally again a week after the race, but during that week you should be content to do easy, relaxed running while your body begins to regenerate its depleted resources.

Chapter 10

Crash Course for the Marathon

There are other views about preparing for a first marathon. The most astonishing of them all comes from Joe Henderson, consulting editor of *Runner's World* magazine, in his book *Jog, Run, Race.* Three months, he writes, is a sufficient prelude for climbing the north face of distance running—the marathon. With certain reservations, the plan is reproduced here. It is typically American and reminds me a little of speed-reading. Just as a speed-reading student devours his three books a week and then finds it impossible to keep them sorted out in his mind, Joe Henderson's blitz course for the marathon also has a few strings attached.

Henderson assumes that the reader is already jogging a half-hour at a time and prescribes an immediate increase to a half-hour a day. For a runner who's been training only two or three times a week, this may be a considerable physical shock. Forsaking the usual gradual increases in mileage, Henderson's plan is certain to result in unforeseen and unpredictable failures of adaptation one time or another during the three months, resulting in chronic muscle soreness and loss of enthusiasm. The step increases in mileage are correct, but the schedule just proceeds at far too quick a pace. In fact, the whole plan resembles a film in accelerated motion. The hard-easy alternation from days of stress to days of easy running is too risky for the beginner as Henderson presents it. The stress of a first hour-long run can stick in a beginner's bones for a whole week. The plan would be commendable if it were stretched out over six months instead of three, beginning with three days a week of running and gradually increasing the number of weekly training days.

Like Henderson, I believe one need not run the marathon distance before the first race. There's no profit in awakening misgivings by encountering the crash point in training. He writes: "Leave the hardest part of the marathon to discover on the day of the race. Then let the other runners help you get through it." But Henderson's short course might lead to the type of marathon experience that has the tortured runner exclaiming at the end, "Never again!"

Only one out of every twenty fun-runners with the ability to run thirty minutes without stopping might actually finish the marathon using this plan. Even if a runner does finish, he won't have done himself any favors. Excess of zeal is harmful in all cases, and the marathon is the quintessential art of waiting. Many runners, attracted by the mystical quality of the marathon, have confided in me that they ran their first marathon too soon, placing excessive stress on themselves and losing ground in their overall progress as runners. Hindsight is wiser than foresight.

Still, Henderson's plan is included here because I feel it will encourage those who think they could never run a marathon. I recommend it unreservedly for athletes who've been active for years and are now coming to the marathon from bicycle racing, cross-country skiing, or swimming. Hardened by their previous training, such athletes will have the conditioning base and mental toughness to go through the program without setbacks.

TABLE 6

Marathon Plan: First Month

Day	Suggested Training
1	25-minute run*
2	25-minute run
3	45-minute run
4	25-minute run

*It is recommended that about 5 percent of each day's run be done at faster than normal pace. This amounts to three minutes per hour.

Table 6 (continued)

5	45-minute run
6	25-minute run
7	Quarter-marathon race or time trial*

Daily average for first week: 34 minutes

8	25-minute run
9	25-minute run
10	50-minute run
11	25-minute run
12	50-minute run
13	25-minute run
14	1:10 run

Daily average for second week: 38 minutes

15	30-minute run
16	30-minute run
17	50-minute run
18	30-minute run
19	50-minute run
20	30-minute run
21	1:20 run

Daily average for third week: 43 minutes

22	30-minute run
23	30-minute run
24	1:00 run
25	30-minute run
26	1:00 run
27	30-minute run
28	1:30 run

*A quarter-marathon is slightly more than 6½ miles.

Table 6 (continued)

Daily average for fourth week: 47 minutes

29	make-up day*
30	make-up day
31	make-up day

Total number of running days for month: 28
Total amount of running for month: 1135 minutes
Average amount of running per day: 40 minutes

TABLE 7

Marathon Plan: Second Month

Day	Suggested Training
1	35-minute run**
2	35-minute run
3	1:10 run
4	35-minute run
5	1:10 run
6	35-minute run
7	10-mile race or time trial

Daily average for first week: 50 minutes

8	35-minute run
9	35-minute run
10	1:10 run
11	35-minute run
12	1:10 run
13	35-minute run
14	1:50 run

*Make up for sessions missed during the month.

**It is recommended you do about 5 percent of each day's run at faster than normal pace. This amounts to three minutes per hour.

Table 7 (continued)

Daily average for second week: 56 minutes

15	40-minute run
16	40-minute run
17	1:20 run
18	40-minute run
19	1:20 run
20	40-minute run
21	2:00 run

Daily average for third week: 63 minutes

22	45-minute run
23	45-minute run
24	1:30 run
25	45-minute run
26	1:30 run
27	45-minute run
28	2:00 run or more

Daily average for fourth week: 69 minutes.

29	make-up day*
30	make-up day
31	make-up day

Total number of running days for month: 28

Total amount of running for month: 1,660 minutes

Average amount of running per day: 59 minutes

*Make up for sessions missed during the month.

TABLE 8

Marathon Plan: Third Month

Day	Suggested Training
1	45-minute run*
2	45-minute run
3	1:30 run
4	45-minute run
5	1:30 run
6	45-minute run
7	Half marathon race or time trial**

Daily average for first week: 64 minutes

Day	Suggested Training
8	45-minute run
9	45-minute run
10	1:30 run
11	45-minute run
12	1:30 run
13	45-minute run
14	2:00 run or more

Daily average for second week: 69 minutes

Day	Suggested Training
15	30-minute run
16	30-minute run
17	1:00 run
18	30-minute run
19	1:00 run
20	30-minute run
21	1:30 run

*It is recommended that you do about 5 percent of each day's run at faster than normal pace. This amounts to 3 minutes per hour.
**A half-marathon is 13.1 miles.

Table 8 (continued)

Daily average for third week: 47 minutes

22	30-minute run
23	30-minute run
24	30-minute run
25	30-minute run
26	30-minute run
27	30-minute run
28	marathon race

Daily average for fourth week: 55 minutes

29	make-up day*
30	make-up day
31	make-up day

Total number of running days for month: 28.

Total amount of running for month: 1650 minutes.

Average amount of running per day: 59 minutes.

*Make up for sessions missed during the month.

Chapter 11

How to Run Under Four Hours

I consider one full year of training the prerequisite for running the marathon in under four hours. Those who've dragged their bodies over the course in five hours would do well to give this precept some thought and begin preparing for their next race more carefully. The under-four-hour aspirant should accustom his body to longer stresses in training and should occasionally go beyond the one-hour training run. During the race the pace will not create a problem. The difficulty will be: metabolic adaptation to long distances; caloric losses; and body heat, water, and electrolyte losses. The first step in meeting these challenges is to run more training miles.

The four-hour marathon runner participates to excess in all the positive and negative phases of the marathon. But the three-hour runner has long since acquired a feeling for rhythm and pace that carries him safely over the distance in more or less routine fashion. The four-hour runner fights a battle with insufficient weapons: one year's preparation after years of living to excess, and the bulk of a heavyweight boxer combined with no objective qualifications for racing long distances except the will to do so. Add to that insufficient metabolic adaptation and lack of racing experience.

How can we make things a little easier for the poor fellow? First off, let us remember the extremely important role played by favorable power-to-weight ratio in the marathon. Tables of caloric losses for the marathon show that the lightweight runner will burn only 2,180 calories in 26 miles, even at a 2:20 pace (given a body weight of 120 pounds). The 220-pound runner requires 3,897 calories to run a 2:54 race—175 percent more energy than the lighter runner. But the heavier runner's metabolic adaptations won't allow him to run this fast in the first place: at a four-hour pace he'll still need half again as much energy as the light-footed 2:20 runner. The heavy runner's body may be capable of converting sufficient calories for a four-hour race if, at 220 pounds, he's at least 6'3" tall. Otherwise, he'll probably have too much passive fat on his body to run four hours.

The above example shows that a runner who wants to finish in an optimal time for his body's abilities should first lose weight. For a heavy-set person, this may take up to a full year. High body weight is a hindrance to running, and keeps a person from running fast enough to make his body lose weight quickly. Also, his weight probably comes from a healthy appetite that he won't be able to throttle from one day to the next. Even if our 200-pounder isn't very interested in food after a forty-five-minute trot through the woods, his digestive juices will certainly announce the presence of hunger before lunchtime the following day. Whenever he tries to eat less, he'll feel a "hole" in his stomach from having stretched his stomach walls more than the normal person's. So it may take many months until he's lost significant weight through running. The runner should be happy if his weight losses are proportional to his accumulated training mileage.

Take a look at pictures of marathon runners. An experienced observer immediately recognizes the class of runner shown in the picture, regardless of when or where it was taken. Stride is one indicator, but physical appearance is much more significant. The beanstalks run at the front; the pumpkins bring up the rear. The front-runner pats himself on the hip at the starting line and says to himself, having felt no fat there at all, "You're in fast shape today, my boy." So, let the normal consumer pay heed. "Down with the pounds" is the marathoner's most important motto. Each pound lost is several minutes gained.

If you come close to your ideal weight and have a 10,000-meter best time of about 46 minutes, you should be able to run under four hours. If you're ten percent or more over your ideal weight, training and dieting will be your pathways to success.

The four-hour runner is not yet a true marathoner. For this reason, he should not push himself in training the way a three-hour runner would. Of course, it would be possible to copy the three-hour runner's training schedules and just run everything slower. But I feel it's wiser for the four-hour runner to reach his time goal in the race before increasing his mileage. Orthopedic injuries occur with great frequency in four-hour runners if they try to go too fast in training or attempt to run too many miles. Bad knees, sciatica, strained ligaments, and even stress fractures occur more frequently in four-hour marathoners than in any other group of runners.

Blind ambition is a common quality among youngsters—even "youngsters" over forty who attempt long-distance running for the first time. Although there is a great incentive to go farther or to keep up with a fast training group, this sort of thing should not become a continual drain on one's powers. Only through years of experience will the runner begin to roll naturally off the ball of his foot when he runs, and will leg and back muscles be sufficiently strengthened and bones correspondingly padded to avoid injury.

I'll proceed on the assumption that the runner is already doing about thirty-five to forty miles a week, with an increase in the last weeks before the marathon. I advise the four-hour runner to enter just three or four races a year, and instead to concentrate on races of fifteen to twenty miles. This will have a positive effect on runners of this class: better sixty miles of racing in shorter events than one marathon too many. Otherwise there's a risk of overstress and slower times from one race to the next, of falling into a monotonous pace and a lifeless stride, and never getting any faster. This may be positive if it happens to a sixty-year-old marathoner whose best times are behind him, but for the younger runner it must be considered negative.

The four-hour runner should not give a hoot about seasonal buildup and other clever scientific ideas. His training will be linear, increasing three to four weeks before the race and tapering off for two weeks afterward. A four-hour runner should allow at least two weeks between races. Although he's not yet quick to recover, he compensates for this with a slow stride that requires less muscle effort and involves much less hard pounding.

After the initial conditioning period, the four-hour runner is less susceptible to muscle stress than the 2:20 runner whose feet bang on the pavement in fast rhythm.

The four-hour runner should not plan his main conditioning for the period from November to May, but should choose the path of least resistance. Assuming he's never done regular winter training, he'll probably run two or three times a week during the colder months, and will have total lapses when he's either too busy or it's too cold or wet. With the arrival of spring, he'll once again take pleasure in running on dry roads and will feel like training regularly. If a fellow runner now talks a four-hour marathoner into running a marathon in the first weeks of May, it may finish him for another six weeks, if not for the whole season. So if you're a four-hour marathoner, make your racing plans for the fall.

Though warm weather helps a runner lose weight, it's best to slow down a little when faced with midsummer heat. Light running clothes improve the runner's style and free him to enjoy the movements of the sport. Long evening runs increase the runner's pleasure, and vacations help him extend his energy into other physical activity.

If you start off in April with an hour's run three times a week, you'll be doing about the right amount. In May, keep running three or four times a week for an hour, and add an occasional fun-run of six miles or longer. Beginning in June, you should include at least one long run of fifteen miles every week, keeping it slow—no faster than two hours. One other weekly training run should exceed an hour.

If you live in an area that gets very hot in July and August, try to run in the mornings or the late evenings, and shorten your distances. An hour's run at 80 to 90 percent effort is much more effective than a tortured attempt to run twenty miles when it's 90 degrees in the shade. Short endurance runs morning and evening during the summer months are unquestionably preferable to long, hot runs. Protect yourself while running in the heat: stick to the shadows and run under thick foliage if you can, or run by the ocean or on a high mountain plateau.

Direct race preparation begins in September. The third week before your marathon might look like this:

Monday	2 x 6 miles in 57 minutes, 20-minute break (15-minute warm-up jog)
Tuesday	Rest
Wednesday	1½ hours of easy endurance running
Thursday	15 miles on the road in about 2:20
Friday	Rest
Saturday	1-hour easy run
Sunday	3-hour forest run with a 5-minute break every hour as desired

This last run is a stress-test, as it comes two weeks before the marathon. It should be followed by three days of recovery, and then perhaps a 12½-mile run in 1:50. For the rest of the training days until the race, do only easy one-hour endurance runs, which may be shortened during the final week.

I do not advise the four-hour runner or the beginning marathoner to go out and run twenty-two miles or longer before the race.

You should not try to run through the crash point in training, because your margin of conditioning will be too thin and it will take you too long to recover. The crash point comes when the body switches over from burning glycogen to burning fats. You can never tell when it will come. For runners in this category, the crash point is largely determined by weather and pacing. If you pace yourself at forty-five minutes for every five miles you'll get through the course with a cushion of six minutes for the last six miles. But you can't depend on getting splits if you're running a four-hour race, as there may be little interest in calling them out at the checkpoints by the time you arrive. It is best to wear a wristwatch and make your own calculations. It is not recommended that a friend run along with you and "help pull you through." This may work for running under three hours, but at a four-hour pace, you may end up wondering if, with this kind of help, you need enemies. After the crash point, no one is going to be able to help you. It's far more reassuring to have a faithful assistant waiting at the last aid stops with a sponge, a cup of electrolyte replacement drink, and a few kind words of encouragement.

Chapter 12

How to Run Under Three Hours

Anyone with sights set on running a three-hour marathon should first serve a three-year apprenticeship as a runner. He should train consistently through an entire winter before the marathon season. If this is not the case, breaking the fabled 3-hour barrier will be difficult. The exception to the rule indicates great talent and—provided the last drop hasn't been squeezed from the grape—speaks of continued improvement for years to come.

To run the marathon in three hours requires year-in, year-out training at a level of 50 to 65 miles a week, spread over five running days. More miles will surely bring the runner over the hurdle, but I would caution against pushing oneself too hard. Training and racing should always be considered a unity. If you place too much stress on your body while training, you may pay the price with an ebb in energy in the middle of a race. Yet if you run too little, you'll never get through either. The great army of runners who are now breaking three hours are proof of the effectiveness of modern endurance training.

The runner in the three-hour category should have a 10,000-meter best time of thirty-six or thirty-seven minutes. If his time is not this good, a sub-three-hour marathon is still theoretically possible, but he'll have to put in considerably more training miles. This is generally worthwhile only for a woman whose previous sub-three-hour times place her among the world's best and who must run daily, seventy-five miles a week, to achieve her time goals.

A runner with considerably more talent, who's increasing from shorter racing distances, will need to place special emphasis on longer training runs—doing more of them while using moderation in applying his natural gift of speed. This might be the case with a junior runner who's run 10,000 meters in thirty-three minutes and now wants to run the marathon, or a forty-two-year-old veteran with a 10,000-meter best of thirty-six minutes who's planning a sub-three-hour marathon in the coming year. Each case demands a different, individualized training plan. I would advise the junior runner to include more cross-country in the winter season and to do only one or two time trials on the road. I would advise the veteran runner to do little cross-country running, and to concentrate on road running from the first day of training until the day of the race.

The woman previously mentioned would require yet another program. She would have to attempt to improve her 10,000-meter time by doing tempo runs of two to three miles.

The following is the general outline of a training plan for the period of November to May.

November. After two weeks of active recovery at the end of October, winter training begins with five hour-long endurance runs per week. The pace should be in the region of 7 to 7½ minutes per mile. If it's so cold that you have to wear a sweater and a jacket, or if the terrain is difficult, you can slow down by a half-minute per mile. In all cases these should be easy, steady endurance runs in which the pulse does not rise beyond 140 beats per minute.

December. The pace remains the same, but try to run seventy minutes three days a week. A race is recommended for the start of the month and again at the end of the year, when so many racing opportunities are available. You should run these races faster than endurance-training pace even though you will be racing with no special preparation. If you have no racing opportunities or do not desire to race, it is advisable to loosen up with an eighty-minute fartlek-style run, with speed changes.

January. The same rule applies here as for the 2:20 to 2:40 runner: never let yourself become overheated during the coldest part of the year. Run seventy-minutes, five days a week, at November's pace for a slight overall increase in training mileage.

One or two forest or cross-country races are appropriate.

February In Europe, this is the cross-country month. Racing is recommended for the younger runner, but no more than three times a month. In your endurance running, you should do an occasional 3,000-meter run in eleven minutes (about two miles in twelve minutes) on the track or on a measured flat course on paths or on the road. Tuesday is a good day for this if you're racing cross-country, since this gives you sufficient time for a little recovery and preparation. If you're a noncompetitor, a warm weekend day would be better for your 3,000-meter run. If you're not racing, don't forget to do fartlek workouts.*

March. At the end of cross-country season, we find ourselves well along in the conditioning period for the marathon. Running clothes are lighter in this season, and the pace quicker. A typical week would look like this (though it is different between races):

Monday	8½-mile endurance run on flat course in 1 hour
Tuesday	1½-hour endurance run of about 11 miles
Wednesday	Rest
Thursday	1:10 endurance run of about 10 miles
Friday	Rest
Saturday	16-mile road run in shoes you'll race in— about 2 hours, no less
Sunday	30-minute warm-up, then 3 x 2 miles in 12 minutes

April. At the end of March or the beginning of April you should enter a road race. It would be ideal to race fifteen and eighteen miles with a two-week interval between, aiming for times around 1:45 and 2:05, respectively. If you run these times without pressing your limits, this indicates your goal is within reach. If you don't succeed in meeting these times, don't give up. You may be the kind of typical "spring runner" who needs a few races to find his rhythm after a winter of

---

* Fartlek training involves running at various speeds over forest trails, parks, and the countryside at will.

running in heavy clothing and cold weather. You may be organically in good condition, but not ready yet to translate your abilities into a good race. During this most important month of all, you should try to get up to sixty-five miles a week, running six or seven days a week if necessary.

Here is a typical week's training for the third week before a marathon race in May:

Monday	8½-mile endurance run in one hour
Tuesday	1:30 fartlek (faster segments of 5 to 15 minutes)
Wednesday	Relaxed 1½-mile run on paths
Thursday	2 x 3 miles on track, 20 minutes each
Friday	8½-mile endurance run in 1 hour
Saturday	15½-mile road run in about 1:55
Sunday	Warm-up, 10 x 880 in about 3:30 to 3:35, with five- to seven-minute breaks in between

May. See the separate section dealing with the two weeks preceding the marathon race. The race should be scheduled for the first half of May because of the pleasantly cool weather that can be expected in many parts of the world at that time of year. Plan your splits using the pacing tables, allowing for thirty-four-minute, five-mile segments. This is a little faster than three-hour marathon pace, so you'll have a certain margin for unforeseen events after the twenty-mile mark.

If your attempt at breaking three hours should fail, I advise taking a break of at least five or six weeks before running another marathon. If you've raced at the beginning of May, try it again in the middle of June. It is no use trying for a personal best time in the summer heat; it is better to start building again for a race in September or October. Endurance running should not be neglected during the summer. I recommend regular racing in fun-runs of about six miles, as well as occasional track races.

Chapter 13

How to Run Under 2:40

The marathoner in the 2:40 class has a training mileage of sixty-five to eighty-five miles a week tattooed on his heels. He will run six or seven days a week, and yet still does not take things quite as seriously as the 2:20 runner. He trains with less intensity and for shorter distances than the 2:20 runner, yet is generally enthusiastic about competition. This is precisely where he may need to exercise a little control. Unlike the sub-2:20 runner, the 2:40 marathoner is unable to run an easy marathon at one outing, and then gallop on to win the next. The 2:40 marathoner has always strong competition within his category, and as a result must run all-out for his times and places. A second danger for the 2:40 runner is the magnetic pull of a strong training partner—a danger that often afflicts an entire group of runners. Frequently, the only good races to come out of such a group are run by the elitist, while the others are the water boys—good running buddies who "left it all on the road" while doing too much of a good thing.

The 2:40 man has neither the talent nor the basic speed and flexibility of the 2:20 runner. His best 10,000-meter times will lie between thirty-two and thirty-three minutes if he has good endurance. He's been at it for years; he's an old racing fox. Running doesn't bring such a runner any profits beyond fitness and experience. He's in the middle-age-group and can perhaps look forward to Master's victories when he's over forty. Still he runs with great enthusiasm and is continually on the track of some new training method, a faster shoe style, or a better liniment.

It's no good giving the 2:40 runner just any old training plan. We'll have to offer him something he can follow to the nearest minute, a schedule that will lead him to within a second or two of his desired goal of precisely 2:40:15.

An ideal example of the training of a 2:40 runner is Christa Vahlensieck's preparation for her first women's world marathon record in 1975. She has run two other 2:40s, but she had her best-ever training and form during the winter of 1975. She was also free of any sickness or injury during that time, which is a further recommendation for her methods. Christa's training schedules can be followed by a man because despite the known male-female differences we've already discussed, conditioning methods and the time for a given racing distance are generally the same for men and women.

However, if I'd been coaching a man instead of Christa Vahlensieck, I would have assigned more runs of about nineteen to twenty-two miles. I would have omitted some of the hard days with two running sessions in favor of one run a day. This is because Christa had an easier time handling twice-a-day workouts than a man would. She weighs only 106 pounds and, as a woman, had better initial hormonal conditions for endurance running. Due to her world-class status in women's marathoning she could run hard twice a day, making her comparable to the sub-2:20 male runner. She has a corresponding level of physical and mental toughness. The 2:40 male, on the other hand, generally has slightly above-average talent. If he could comfortably assimilate Christa's training plan verbatim, he would very soon improve to 2:35.

Christa was twenty-six years old in 1975. She had run long distances from early childhood, coached by Adam Rosenbaum. She always raced the longest available distances—first 1,500, then 3,000 meters. On October 28, 1973, she ran the first marathon ever held for women only, at Waldniel, West Germany, and won in a European best time of 2:59:25.6 to the immense satisfaction of the organizer, Dr. Ernst van Aaken.

Her next marathon was a 2:53 in 1974 at Boston, where she finished second to Miki Gorman. Then in the first women's marathon championship race in September 1974 at Waldniel, she ran a rather disappointing 2:54:40 for fourth place. At this point, I again assumed the role of her trainer. I'd coached

Christa with few interruptions since 1969, having helped her to the German 1,500-meter title. On October 26, 1974, Christa ran a 2:42:38, which was first hailed as a world record until remeasurement proved the course was short by 754 meters. The date was significant, however, because from that point on, West German track officials turned greater attention to measuring marathon courses, sharpening the rules, and demanding more care.

Her fast time gave Christa an incentive to attempt a true world record. Christa was not intimidated that Jackie Hansen had run 2:43:54.6 in December 1974 and that Liane Winter had won at Boston in 2:42:33, each setting a new world record. Christa had already set her sights on 2:40. Christa chose the Dulmen Marathon in Germany for her record attempt in May 1975, since it has a near-ideal flat course.

To speak in technical terms, Christa's training was cyclic with double periodization. Dulmen was the high point of the first period, but she also aimed toward a best-possible place and a good time for the German 3,000-meter title race two weeks later. This is why certain elements in her training were planned to improve her times at shorter distances.

In December, Christa's mileage was about sixty-five a week. She was training according to my motto that it's better to run as many miles as possible when the weather allows, but to go the way of least resistance when the weather makes you cut back. An exception in Christa's training was the period around Christmas and New Year's, when numerous days off from work freed her to train in the evenings. A short period of hard training brought her available reserves to the fore and resulted in excellent form. Her training diary entries for the period looked like this:

Sunday, 12/22	2-hour sharp endurance run, about 16.75 miles
Monday, 12/23	6.2 miles easy, followed by 1 x 300 at race pace
Tuesday, 12/24	5 miles before breakfast on paths, 9.3 miles on roads in the afternoon
Wednesday, 12/25	6.2 miles in the morning, 10 miles on roads in the afternoon

Thursday, 12/26	18.5-mile run on a flat course in the woods at moderate pace
Friday, 12/27	6.2-mile easy run
Saturday, 12/28	15.5-mile run on rolling terrain in 2 hours
Sunday, 12/29	5 miles easy in the morning, 9.3 miles on roads in the afternoon
Monday, 12/30	1 hour in the forest and on roads (7.5 to 8.5 miles)
Tuesday, 12/31	6.2 miles easy

While doing this easy running, Christa Vahlensieck could not have dreamed that she'd be running 5.3 miles through the streets of São Paulo, Brazil, on New Year's Eve the next two years, winning the famous midnight run each time. Her training between Christmas and New Year's when added to a winter-long base of long endurance running, had the unintended effect of preparing her for a good racing time. In 1974, though, women were not yet allowed to enter the São Paulo race.

Wednesday, 1/1	3.75 miles in the morning easy; 2 hours in the afternoon on roads, very easy (14-15 miles)
Thursday, 1/2	1-hour run, 2 x 1,000 meters (0.62 miles) sharp in forest
Friday, 1/3	1-hour endurance run (7.5 to 8.5 miles)
Saturday, 1/4	5 miles in morning easy, afternoon 3 x 3 miles on flat forest trails, last loop in 17:30

That was followed by a week of loafing. On January 12, Christa ran a (well-measured) 6.2-mile forest run all-out in fine weather in 34:25. Following this successful time trial, she was able to return the quiet, monotonous pace of daily one-hour endurance runs. Only on weekends, with the opportunity to train in daylight, did she exceed this mileage.

Christa's next test race was on February 9, a 9.3-mile (15-kilometer) event, which she ran faster than planned in an excellent time of 53:21. Her only inconsistency in form during the entire 1975 season was at the district cross-country title race, which she entered as defending champion. She was very nervous about Vera Kemper, a cross-country specialist who was also entered in the race, and dropped out when she was unable to stay with Kemper.

Things looked better on March 1 at the national cross-country championships in Berlin, where Christa deliberatedly ran a slow race at the start and came on strong at the finish. By avoiding oxygen debt in the sand hills, she finished second in 18:27 for the very difficult 4,580-meter course, behind Vera Kemper who won in 17:38.4. In a sudden change of plans, Christa then drove straight from Berlin to a 12.4-mile race in Konigsforst, which she won in 1:15:37. Her training schedule for the day read "one hour of easy running in the woods." Christa assured me this was just what she'd done in the race.

The Konigsforst race was the last of three, forming a winter racing series that Christa won. Her times in these races were:

January 12	10 km.	34:25
February 9	15 km.	53:21
March 1	20 km.	1:15:37
Total:	45 km.	2:43:23

(marathon distance is 42 kilometers)

If you do series of ten-, fifteen-, and twenty-kilometer runs on flat courses, after doing only marathon training, you will almost certainly run a comparable marathon time during the coming season. Christa could have cut three minutes off her final 20-kilometer race, which would have brought the series total even closer to her actual 2:40 marathon time later that year. The racing series in Cologne's Konigsforst Park is, to my mind, ideal preparation for the marathon runner. The distances, course, and dates coincide exactly with the marathoner's needs. It is no coincidence that the races regularly draw up to 1,000 entries.

Returning to the details of Christa's training:

Saturday, 2/22	15.5-mile road run in just under 2 hours

Sunday, 2/23	Warm-up, then flat 2.8-mile loop in woods, fast but not all-out, followed by 3 or 4 hill runs
Monday, 2/24	1-hour road run (8 to 8.75 miles)
Tuesday, 2/25	Track work: 30-minute warm-up, then 3 x 1000 m. (0.62 mi.) in track shorts in 3:10 to 3:15 with 6-minute breaks in between, followed by a long warm-down run
Wednesday, 2/26	1:10 fartlek on varied terrain
Thursday, 2/27	1-hour easy run in woods
Friday, 2/28	Trip to Berlin, 30-minute endurance run on arrival
Saturday, 2/29	German cross-country title race, 4,580 m. in 18:27 for second place
Sunday, 3/1	12.4-mile (20-km.) race in Cologne in 1:15:37

In March, average mileage was increased to seventy-five miles a week. The next race was a 15.5-mile (25-kilometer road event for which we had set a time goal of 1:34. Christa ran a world-record 1:31:52, despite losing valuable seconds at a railroad crossing. By this point, I was convinced Christa could go through the 25-kilometer (15.5-mile) split in the marathon in 1:35. The task that now lay ahead was for Christa to run long to prepare muscles and metabolism to the point where she could maintain a 19-minute 5,000-meter (3.1-mile) pace through the marathon for a finishing time of 2:40:30.

Easter was a focal point for increased mileage due to the available free time and the short time remaining before the record attempt in Dulmen:

Wednesday, 3/26	Track work: 3 x 1,000 m. (0.62 mile) in 3:20 with 5-minute breaks between
Thursday, 3/27	1-hour run in woods
Friday, 3/28	5-mile road run in morning, 8.06-mile run in woods in afternoon (1 hour)
Saturday, 3/29	2½-hour endurance run, about 20.5 miles (longest run of the winter to this point!)

Sunday, 3/30	(Easter) 1-hour run in woods
Monday, 3/31	1-hour road run (9.3 miles)
Tuesday, 4/1	1½-hour fartlek
Wednesday, 4/2	Track work: 5 x 1,000 m. (0.62 mi.) in 3:20
Thursday, 4/3	1-hour easy run in forest
Friday, 4/4	Easy 40-minute run
Saturday, 4/5	9.3-mile Spiridon road race in 56:30 (goal 57 minutes)

The main goal in the Spiridon race was to simulate race pace under competitive conditions. After starting too fast over the first five kilometers, Christa held her pace steady to the finish.

Further training for April, the most important conditioning month:

Sunday, 4/6	½-hour easy run in morning, 1:20 in afternoon
Monday, 4/7	1-hour easy run
Tuesday, 4/8	1½-hour road run, about 12.4 miles
Wednesday, 4/9	6.2-mile endurance run in morning, track work in evening: 3 x 1,000 m. in 3:30 to 3:40; 1 x 5,000 m. in 19 minutes (actually ran 18:18); 2 x 1,000 m. in 3:30 to 3:40 (actually 3:20 and 3:29); 5-minute break between all runs
Thursday, 4/10	1-hour run in woods, pace as desired
Friday, 4/11	5 miles in morning, evening 1:20
Saturday, 4/12	6.2 miles in morning, 2 hours in afternoon (16.1 miles)
Sunday, 4/13	At noon, to get used to starting time of Dulmen marathon, a 2-hour run of about 16 miles on roads
Monday, 4/14	5 miles in morning easy, evening 50 minutes in woods (6.82 miles)
Tuesday, 4/15	1:20 in woods with tempo run at end at race pace
Wednesday, 4/16	6.2-mile run in morning in woods; evening track work: 3 x 3,000 m. (1.86 miles) in 11:25 with 6- to 8-minute breaks

Thursday, 4/17	Easy 8.06-mile run (1 hour)
Friday, 4/18	Easy 8.06-mile run (1 hour)
Saturday, 4/19	2½-hour fartlek run, including walking pauses and phases of 10-30 minutes running at desired pace but never faster than marathon race pace, sprinting uphill and maintaining a flowing, relaxed stride going downhill
Sunday, 4/20	Easy 5-mile run in morning, 1-hour road run on flat course in afternoon for 10 miles at marathon race pace
Monday, 4/21	1-hour easy run
Tuesday, 4/22	24.18-mile run in woods in 3:18

This last run, which we did together, came the day after Liane Winter's world-record race at Boston in 2:42:24. We were already aiming at a 2:40:30 race, but I had to apply the brakes time after time to keep Christa from running too fast. She would have run 3:05 if I'd let her. But that would have defeated the purpose of the run—to tune her metabolism for the Dulmen race by running long.

Christa, at this point, felt a little heavy in the legs and overextended. A week's easy running brought back her strength, and on April 27 she raced 3,000 meters in 9:58. We had scheduled this race using a tactic followed by Frank Shorter and Karel Lismont, of having a shorter race one week before an important marathon.

At Dulmen, Christa's splits were:

5 km.	18:18
10 km.	38:50
15 km.	58:20
20 km.	1:17:05
25 km.	1:35:35
30 km.	1:54:15
35 km.	2:13:02

At 35 kilometers (21.7 miles), Christa was nearly on schedule (2:13:00 was the planned split). She compensated for the slight weakness of running against the wind between kilometers twenty-six and thirty-eight by accelerating over the final two kilometers for a new world-record time of 2:40:15.8. Two weeks later, she ran 3,000 meters in 9:25.6 to place fourth in the German nationals.

An invitation to the international meet with the U.S. women at Durham, run in extreme heat, resulted in a personal best time of 9:14.8. Later in the season, she ran world-record times at 10,000 meters (34:01.6 in Wolfsburg, Germany) and the hour run (16,872.40 meters, in Bochum, Germany). She easily won the first official German women's marathon title race in October in 2:45:43, and ended the year with a victory at the Sao Paulo New Year's Run.

Christa's excursions into the shorter racing distances, resulting in best times, should encourage the young runner who is vacillating between track and road. Such runners will not lose speed by doing marathon training. On the contrary, they will create a base for improved times, even at the shorter distances.

I would warn runners in the 2:40 category not to run with Christa Vahlensieck in a marathon, because at nineteen miles she'll leave you behind. She is among the few runners who are faster over the second half of the marathon. Anton Gorbunov, former German marathon titlist, started fifteen minutes after Christa in the 1976 national championship race, passed her early, and then had to watch helplessly as she easily passed him in the final miles.

When Christa regained her world title (as well as the world record) in September 1977 in Berlin with a 2:34:47.5, her training had not changed significantly. She has maintained the year-round weekly standard of 75 miles, with up to 115 miles during a peak conditioning phase. But she says she's gained pace-toughness by doing more fartlek running. At Berlin, the race conditions were ideal and Christa had a rival who held even with her to the twenty-mile mark (Manuela Angenvoorth).

Training year-after-year for competition is a waste of effort unless the runner keeps increasing her capital—adding quantity as well as quality to her running bank account. This is what Christa has done.

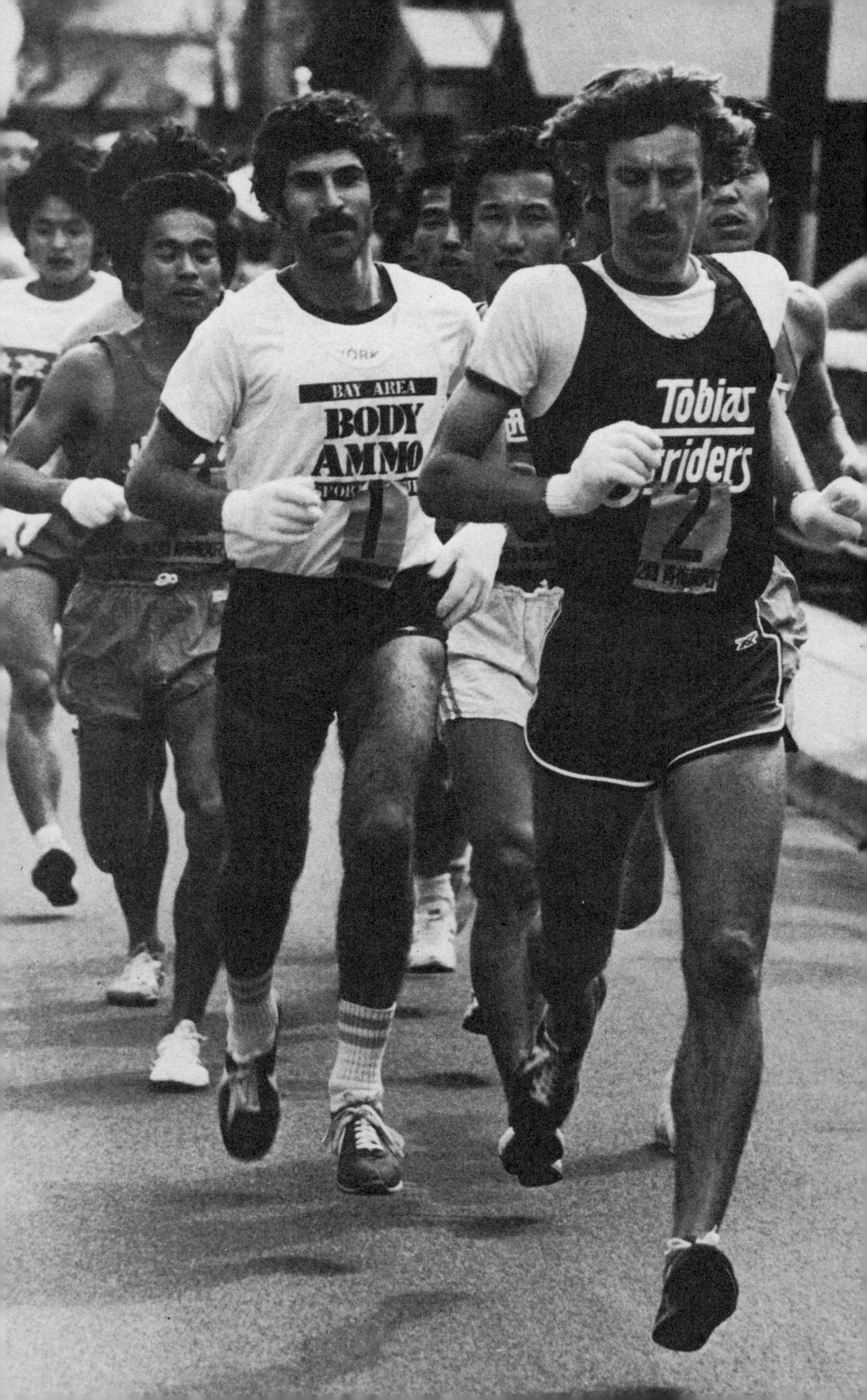
BAY AREA
BODY
AMMO
Tobias

Chapter 14

How to Run Under 2:20

While running the marathon in under 2:20 is no longer the ticket to world-class acclaim, this magic number still entices the top-rank runner who has gone through a 1:47 split for twenty miles and hopes that now he will make a great breakthrough. When the attempt fails, the runner assumes that he either has an incorrigible weakness beyond twenty miles or that he has simply gone out too fast.

It is strange that so many runners remain stuck at 2:22 or 2:23. Most of them do not seek a better placing, but rather a personal best around 2:19. Once the person runs a sub-2:20 marathon, progress is usually so fast that results of 2:15 to 2:18 no longer seem out of reach.

What separates the 2:20 runner from the 2:30 runner? To begin with, the hobby of running now eats up a major proportion of the 2:20 runner's free time. He must train daily, with few exceptions, during the entire year. The 2:20 runner's weekly mileage should range from 75 to at most 150 miles a week. For better distribution of effort, he should run twice a day two or three days a week. The runner must always be in the best of health, not just free of illness, but orthopedically sound. (Something as minor as an infected tooth can interrupt training for as long as six months.) Psychological instability, too, often causes gastrointestinal trouble or side stitches during the racing season, though these problems may of course have completely different organic causes.

The 2:20 runner should keep his family life intact. He must

be able to organize his limited free time so that he doesn't spend too much time running and shrivel up as a person. He must be careful that he doesn't become so obsessed with this area of his life that he turns into a compulsive runner. While these things are equally true for 2:12 runners, they will have previously recorded encouraging times, and thus may be under less mental strain than the runner who is trying to break 2:20 for the first time.

There are, of course, a few gifted runners who've gone under 2:20 in their first marathon, as was the case of Ian Thompson in the British national title race in 1973, which he won in 2:12:40. But statistically this is the absolute exception. In general, we must expect the following qualifications of the person who wants to move into the sub-2:20 category:

- 4 years of systematic base conditioning at the long distances
- 2 to 3 marathons (breakthroughs frequently come in the fourth)
- a 10,000-meter best of under thirty minutes
- about 900-50 miles of training during the eight weeks prior to the race
- a flat course
- temperatures between 45 and 65 degrees F and little wind

Since these factors seldom coincide completely, the runner should make contingency plans well in advance. It is very frustrating for example, to look forward to a race and then not enter because of hot weather. In such a situation it is best to be satisfied with a decent place and then to wait for more favorable racing conditions.

The Typical Sub-2:20 Runner

Runner's World magazine made a survey of forty American sub-2:20 runners. Since the United States leads the world in marathoning, the values obtained are applicable to other areas of the world, as well. They are, in any case, more interesting than the data obtained from Olympic runners in 1972 and 1976, since these runners came from substantially different cultures and represented varying physical characteristics and histories. Seventy percent of the runners questioned were married; of these, 80 percent had no children. They averaged

25.2 years of age, but the average absolute peak-class runner was about four years older. Twenty-three percent were teachers by profession and thirty percent were students. All this data indicates that these runners have living or occupational conditions that provide free time for devoting an enormous amount of attention to the marathon. In fact, 13 percent gave "sporting goods dealer" as their occupation. We can assume that many of these runners sell shoes and other training gear out of the trunks of their cars (as did former European marathon champion Ron Hill of Great Britain, though Hill, with a Ph. D. in chemistry, was working a regular forty-hour-a-week job at the time). Only about a third of the runners surveyed work a normal eight-hour day. Even among these the canvas is colorful: there is a helicopter pilot, a policeman, a steelworker, a male nurse, and even a sailor who runs his miles on a carrier flight deck (twenty-eight-year-old Phil Camp, who ran 2:18:06 in 1976).

The forty U.S. marathoners with the best times under 2:20 average 5'8½" in height and weigh 136 pounds. During the two months prior to their best respective races, they averaged 800 miles in training, ranging from a minimum of 100 miles in the case of an injured runner to a high of 1,090 miles. The average highest-mileage week was 119 miles. On the average, the runners did 3.8 runs of more than twenty miles in the eight weeks prior to the race; the single longest run was twenty miles. Seventy-four percent of the training miles were run at slower than race pace, and 88 percent did track work using intervals. Half of the runners were injured at least part of the time in the eight weeks preceding the race. Most runners ran their best race in their eleventh attempt, and 80 percent ran their best race on even splits. Most of them had begun running at age fifteen or sixteen, but their first marathon averaged a relatively poor 2:48. In contrast to European runners, who come to the roads from the track, American runners tend to go directly into road events at a much earlier age. One of the runners reported a 4:30 first marathon!

The best times of the sub-2:20 Americans at other distances are also of interest: 100 yards in 11.7, 440 yards in 54.1, mile in 4:13, 3 miles in 13:52, 6 miles in 29:00. To conclude, these are the points that America's top-class runners gave as the decisive factors in their success:

- regularity
- hard training
- mental attitude
- long runs
- combined types of training

In the group surveyed, only one runner said he ran for physical fitness. For these runners, athletic ambition is the deciding motivation. Among four-hour runners things would certainly be reversed.

Preparation for Race Day

Given average temperate weather conditions, we can assume that ideal racing weather will prevail with certainty only in April, May, September, and October. Happily, after many years of stagnation, the championship races and other important events in Germany are now usually scheduled at these times of the year. In 1971 the German National was still held in early July, in the plains of the Lower Rhine region where you can bet hard currency on having a hot day. In fact, it was 86 degrees F in the shade at the 6 p.m. starting time.

So as not to make the yearly training schedule too complicated, as it includes a double cycle, let's plan for a race at the beginning of May. Preparation for the race begins in the month of October. Training for the period between October and February will be presented here in its broad outlines.

October. Let's assume that the last marathon of the previous season was run in September or October. It won't usually have been run on a sufficient training base, but is completed on deep reserves and routine training. Even though early fall, with its clear days and turning leaves, is one of the prime running seasons of the year, rest and regeneration are urgently needed. Only one with no recent hard racing stresses behind him can safely take advantage of the weather to "eat miles." Others should be satisfied with sixty-five miles a week on a run per day, with at most one weekend day of two workouts. Total abstinence from racing is recommended.

November. Although the days are shorter and the paths soft and slippery, November is an important month for conditioning mileage. If there's frequent morning fog, the runner may have to content himself with one workout a day and reduce his pace. Training runs should be at least 1:00 to 1:15, at a 6:45 pace. At least twice a week, go on runs of 17 to 18 ½ miles in 2:00 to 2:10. In this way the total mileage is brought up to 90 to 100 miles per week.

December. The European cross-country season begins in December, and the marathon runner should participate with ambition. This is the time when toughness is acquired and when leg muscles and thick capillary networks are developed by continuous changes in stride and varied terrain. Along with racing, training mileage is also further increased. On the Saturday before a Sunday race the runner should run easy. After a cross-country race the runner should go out on Monday and run twelve to fifteen miles.

In December, the runner should take advantage of vacation days for increased training. Over the Christmas holidays, when traffic is light, the runner can go out and do relatively fast training runs during the daylight hours. At a pace of 6:00 to 6:20 per mile, weekly mileage should reach 110 miles, including cross-country races.

January. During the coldest month of the year, training mileage should not continue to increase in linear fashion. The runner who pushes his mileage to record heights in January, as was once prescribed by classical training theory, will be lucky to get through without suffering reverses. Exaggerated effort in January can later lead to sciatica, rheumatic complaints, or infections of the lower urinary tract. The best policy is to go the way of least resistance, holding onto December's form, varying one's training as much as the weather allows, and if need be, dropping back to seventy-five to ninety miles a week. Practice shows that a fairly fast cross-country race on the weekend, say 10,000 meters, with a shower shortly after the race, is less strength-sapping than a two-hour run in steady rain or below-freezing temperatures in sweaty clothes that have become cold and clammy.

February. European weather in February follows no strict pattern, but you can assume that average running conditions will be a little better than in January. The days begin to get longer, strengthening the desire to run more miles. Racing includes important cross-country events, especially national-title races, which are commonly held around the first of the month. The runner should not try to race every weekend, however, but should be more concerned with keeping his weekly mileage around ninety.

If the weather is bad, there's no other way to get through February than to grit one's teeth and keep running, as the planned ebb in the yearly training cycle is scheduled for January. The racing season is too close now to think of taking it easy. But here, too, take the route of least resistance. Train whenever possible, taking advantage of times when it's warm, as well as the daylight hours between 11 a.m. and 2 p.m. on weekends.

March. In March, the farmer hitches his team to the plow. Similarly, this is the time for the marathon runner to put effort into training. If you expect to be in super condition by the beginning of May, April will have to be one of the year's big mileage months.

The runner who has been racing enthusiastically during cross-country season and still isn't quite geared to training for the roads will have to schedule marathons for a little later. He might wait until the end of May or sometime in June, though by then he'll risk encountering less than optimal racing weather. Training mileage approaching 550 is not too much for March.

The following is a schedule for the eight weeks from March until the first race:

1st Week

	Morning	Afternoon
Monday	6.2 mi. easy	18.4 mi. in woods 1:15
Tuesday		15.5 mi. in woods easy
Wednesday	9.3 mi. under 1:00	9.3 mi. under 1:00
Thursday	5 mi. easy	13.6 mi. on road 1:30
Friday		9.3 mi. easy
Saturday	12.4 mi. fartlek	12.4 mi. on road 1:10-1:15
Sunday	5 mi. easy	18.6 mi. in woods 2:00

2nd Week

Monday		12.4 mi. in woods 1:15

	Morning	*Afternoon*
Tuesday	9.3 mi. under 1:00	9.3 mi. under 1:00
Wednesday	6.2 mi. easy	12.4 mi. in woods 1:15
Thursday	9.3 mi easy in woods	12.4 mi. on roads 1:15
Friday		9.3 mi. fartlek
Saturday	15.5 mi. road 1:40	
Sunday	Cross-country race (6.2 - 8.68 mi.), 3mi. warm-down	

3rd Week

Monday		12.4 mi easy in woods
Tuesday	9.3 mi. under 1·00	9.3 mi. under 1:00
Wednesday	6.2 mi. easy	12.4 mi. on roads 1:15
Thursday	9.3 mi. easy	10.5-11.6 mi. in 1:00
Friday		15.5 mi. fartlek
Saturday	6.2 mi. easy	18.6 mi. on road 1:50
Sunday	12.4 mi. easy in woods	12.4 easy in woods

4th week

Monday		track: 8 x 0.62 mi. in 3:20; rest 1:30; run total of 12.4 mi.
Tuesday		18.6 mi. easy in woods
Wednesday	9.3 mi. easy	12.4 mi. in 1:15
Thursday	9.3 mi. easy	track: 5 x 200 m. 35.0; 2,000 m. (1.24 mi.) 6:30; 5 x 200 m. 35.0; 2,000 m. 6:30; run 5 series with a 5-min. break after each 2,000-m. run
Friday		15.5 mi. easy
Saturday	18.6 mi. on road 1:50	
Sunday	12.4 mi. easy in woods	12.4 mi. easy on roads

5th Week

Monday		18.6 mi. in woods
Tuesday		10.5-11.6 mi. in 1:00
Wednesday		18.6 mi. in woods
Thursday		20.5 mi. on roads 2:00-2:05

	Morning	*Afternoon*
Friday		11.6 mi. easy
Saturday		9.3 mi. easy
Sunday	Cross-country race of 6.2-8.7 mi. (10,000-15,000 m.)	

(This week there is only one run a day in order to give the runner a psychological rest.)

6th Week

	Morning	Afternoon
Monday		9.3 mi. easy
Tuesday		track: 2 x 5,000 m. (3.1 mi.) in 15:30, 10 to 15-min. breaks; 30-min. warm-up and warm-down runs
Wednesday		15.5 mi. easy fartlek
Thursday		11.6 mi. easy in woods
Friday		6.2 mi. on roads in 35-38 min.
Saturday	15.5 mi. road race (goal 1:19) or 18.6 mi. in 1:36:30	

(This race is considered a test of marathon condition.)

Sunday	6.2 mi. easy	6.2 mi. relaxed and easy

7th Week

	Morning	Afternoon
Monday	rest day	
Tuesday	6.2 mi. easy	12.4 mi. on roads 1:15
Wednesday	9.3 mi. easy	15.5 mi. easy
Thursday	9.3 mi. easy	track: 3,000 m. (1.7 mi.) in 8:50
Friday		21.7 mi. in 2:20 on roads and in woods
Saturday	9.3 mi. easy	10.5 mi. in 1:00
Sunday	Three-hour aerobic run, 18.6 mi.	

8th Week

Monday		15.5 mi. in 1:40
Tuesday		6.2 mi. on roads in 33:00

	Morning	Afternoon
Wednesday	9.3 mi. in 1:00	track: 50 x 100 m. in 18 sec., jog back
Thursday	rest day	
Friday		easy 15 mi. in 2:00
Saturday	marathon race with goal of running under 2:20	

The times given in the schedules assume flat terrain. If the training area has a varied topography, the times will have to be adjusted. The fast one-hour runs should be done on flat ground if possible to help the runner acquire steady rhythm for the race. It isn't stated in many instances whether the running surface should be forest paths or roads. This is left for the runner to decide, depending on available routes and the runner's feelings. But the runner will not succeed in road racing without training on the roads. Only runners who can never train on hard surfaces without experiencing foot or knee problems should avoid running on roads. In these cases, a terrible-sounding but effective rule may help: "When it hurts, go faster." The reason for this is that fast running demands a more economical style, which alters the body's working level relationships to bypass possible sources of pain.

The Six- to Eight-Week Break

Any further increases in mileage after the last weekend of April will be difficult. Year after year you see it happen: the outsider runs a great race in spring, then enters a national-championship or team-selection marathon and flops. There is a great art to holding one's form throughout the summer while constantly improving it.

Track races at 5,000 and 10,000 meters often conflict with periods set aside for important heavy training. As far as possible, the runner should continue to do marathon training and run track races on this base alone. For example, the following is a weekly training schedule for a marathoner who wants to attempt a 1,500-meter time of under four minutes the following Sunday:

Monday	18.6 mi. in two sessions
Tuesday	morning, 9.2 easy mi.; afternoon, track: 5 x 400 m. in 64, followed by an easy 6.8-mi. run
Wednesday	morning 6.2-mi. endurance run; afternoon, 9.3-mi. fartlek with short, fast sections
Thursday	track: 3 x 2,000 m. (1.24 mi.) in 6:00, followed by 1 x 300 m. in 40-42 sec.
Friday	15.5 mi. in woods in 1:40
Saturday	easy endurance run of 18.6 mi.
Sunday	1,500-m. race

While this bit of track preparation serves as a relaxing diversion in the marathoner's program, it does not detract from training in any way. There is no purpose in doing the specific training of a 1,500-meter runner, which would merely cause hyperacidification and produce negative results in a race.

Between marathon races there should, in principle, be a complete pause from racing for six to eight weeks. Four or, at most, five race entries per year are plenty for the runner of this category, since his training load already has him working at near optimal stress levels. More racing is advised only if the runner plans a winter marathon for conditioning, which will be run at a slow pace.

Around the middle of June, there are usually plenty of good, fast races. Many international races are held in August. The key is to hold one's form—to find a balanced relationship between speed and endurance—and to adapt to the heat as well. An August race spells an early season's end for many runners who find themselves in a state of chronic physical and psychological depletion. Their times are likely to be far beneath their potential. This is why it so often happens that the methodical second-rank runner who has carefully prepared for a single important fall race will be able to beat the stars in that event. Such a runner is at a mental peak, keyed for this one race. He generally has just enough reputation to unsettle the faster, but tired, youngsters when they see him going strong at eighteen or twenty miles.

The sub-2:20 runner should be particularly careful not to let himself fall into the trap of neglecting long slow distance during the summer. The fizz is often more important than the gin. Any bartender knows the trick of mixing drinks that are strong enough to please the customer, but are not so strong that they get him drunk too quickly. It's the task of the coach or the self-coached runner to mix his medicine with care.

Another error, less frequently seen, leads just as surely to a crisis. This is where the long runs become too fast in summer as the runner sheds clothes and begins to feel his oats. Hot weather spells high electrolyte losses, which often are not recognized until it's too late. A good rule of thumb is to run long ones a little faster in summer, but to cut down accordingly on the total mileage.

Looking at 2:10 and Under

What's the difference between the 2:20 marathoner and the international-class competitor with a best time of 2:12, 2:10, or faster? One difference is natural talent. The best 10,000-meter time, for a sub-2:10 marathoner will be close to a flat twenty-eight minutes. Such a runner will weigh little more than 130 pounds, and will consequently have an excellent power-to-weight ratio for low-calorie consumption at racing speeds. This factor may actually be more important in daily training than it is for racing.

The world-class runner does not race with great frequency. He will not become diverted from well-thought-out training plans by any second-rate marathon that he could win walking. Frank Shorter and Karel Lismont are two good examples of runners who use this pattern of selective racing. They both compete with regularity only at the shorter distances—Shorter at two miles to 5,000 meters and Lismont in winter cross-country races and road races up to the half-marathon. Otherwise, they both prefer a premiere without a dress rehearsal. The same was true of Abebe Bikila (perhaps the greatest marathon runner in history); Canada's Jerome Drayton; Derek Clayton: and, in his best years, Ron Hill. When Hill passed the zenith of his running career, he became a 2:15 runner who could be found at races from Szeged, Hungary, to Baltimore. In his peak years, he protested even the requirement of an Olympic qualifying marathon, for he preferred to put all his resources into the first and, if possible, the only race of the year.

These are a few minor points, but they show the exactitude with which runners at the top try to balance the total stress loads of training and racing. They renounce lesser victories and acclaim while hiding in the anonymity of their private lives, to emerge for the one great marathon race with international status. They run few races and train for many miles. During most of the year they'll run over 125 miles a week; but for racing at this level, the upper limit seems to be about 150 miles a week or 600 a month. Rhythm makes the music: a little faster all the time, with occasional dazzling bursts of speed.

A factor of extraordinary significance at the sub-2:12 level is the arrangement of one's personal affairs so that the marathon has absolute priority over studies and other activities. An eight-hour work day is simply impossible with this level of stress. The only way to preserve psychic reserves is to have plenty of free time. Optimal control of one's hours allows training to be spread out more than was the case in the training plans for the sub-2:20 runner. One hour, 3 times a day is a better rhythm than twenty miles in a single outing at race pace. Both are borderline stresses, but the runner who trains three times a day is less vulnerable to overtraining and injury than the one who must train in a single daily effort. From the point of view of speed and distance, the runner will actually be doing more in three runs than his opponent who must do all his training in one long run.

Training is rarely that simple. Only a generously subsidized world-class runner can plan on consistent, optimal daily workouts. Only he can follow the wise adage: for every hour of work, an hour of rest. The eight-hour worker is forced to steal running minutes from his hours of sleep. The soldier in an army special services athletic outfit or the student with a light class load can nap at midday, and if worries about his occupational future do not cause him undue stress, he'll be two or three minutes faster for his daily snooze.

The best training areas in the world are available to the sub-2:12 runner at the best times of year. (One immediately thinks of Finland's Lasse Viren.) The sub-2:12 runner will have the best doctors, the best races to enter, and the best shoes made from patterns of his own feet and replaced every 150 miles. He'll have gammaglobulin shots to immunize him against flu, electrolyte drinks prepared for his own specific sweat losses, special diets, and X-rays to tell him how far to run if his foot or tendon is injured. When he races, he's ready.

General training plans don't even exist at this level. The sub-2:12 marathoner should do more runs, at a faster pace, and higher mileage than the 2:20 runner; this is as close as we can come to a general formula. The world-class runner will need customized running shorts, since clothes off the rack do not meet his needs. In expertise and intuition, he'll be far above most of the world's coaches. This may also be why socialist marathon collectives have seldom had success at international competitions. The only exceptions are Russia's 1958 European champion Popov and East Germany's 1976 Olympic gold medalist Waldemar Cierpinski. We know, however, that the East Germans' success is based largely on general abandonment of athletic collectives in favor of individual handling of top athletes within a team structure. In the case of Cierpinski, a steeplechase man who gradually worked his way up to the marathon attained absolute peak condition in the summer of 1976. Even before the 1976 Games marathon, Cierpinski astonished his opponents with his ability to train at a fast pace with no sign of overexertion.

Rumors of blood doping, expressed in the cases of Viren and Cierpinski, must be refuted.* Highly trained distance runners just don't do this kind of thing; it's the last resort of athletes in certain other sports disciplines who are desperately trying to compensate for deficits in condition. Dr. Aloys Mader, formerly an official advisor to East German world-class athletes and now a resident of Cologne, West Germany, has rejected the use of drugs by Cierpinski: "If East Germany had found a performance improving medication for the marathon, they would never have shown up at Montreal with just one runner. They'd have sent three and all three would have placed well."

There is a definite contrast between the front-runner and the average plodder in the marathon. It is a fundamental difference of nature, but it should never be allowed to degenerate into open rivalry. We need both types in the marathon; huge fields of plodders and the outstanding winning marathoners. These

*Blood doping involves returning to a runner's body up to a liter of blood which has been withdrawn several weeks before a major race.

two groups are the most important ones in a marathon race. The world-class runner should not stand at the finish line of a marathon, commenting contemptuously on the arrival of the "legion of the varicose-veined." Similarly, the average runner should still his objections to the token entry fee that goes toward the international-class runner's plane fare and expenses. Both groups depend on each other.

The plodder fills an important function, which I became aware of during the pre-Olympic 10,000-meter race at Munich in 1971. The next-to-last finisher, Lucien Rosa of Ceylon, turned around at the end of the race and enthusiastically shook my hand, as I came in last. Rosa, who later became a front-runner in the U.S., was grateful to finish ahead of someone, and by his friendly attitude he sweetened my disappointment. The first must accept the last. After all, excellence can be identified only by contrast with the average.

So, if you're looking for the recipe for a world-record race, I must remind you of the sacrifices of the world-class runner. No marathon runner of the world class will ever become rich solely from his sport. In fact, in the interest of maintaining good form he declines most offers to race. The few races that are lucrative for him give him no more than a few nice trips and expense money several times a year. There is seldom enough cash left over for more than a couple of weeks of ordinary living expenses. The world-class runner trains 1,000 hours a year. If he were to make $4,000 a year from his racing, he would be earning the salary of a temporary office worker. But the world-class runner rarely makes that much because he'll be paying in other ways out of his own pocket for his running.

The world-class runner who does accept travel and public acclaim as his highest goals should have the tolerance to fully accept his colleagues at the other end of the racing spectrum.

Part Three

Eating and Drinking for Fast Times

Chapter 16

The Marathoner's Diet

Your diet has an extremely important effect on your running and racing. Three phases of diet concern the marathoner:

- normal, everyday diet
- diet just before and during races
- diet after the all-out stresses of racing

The second phase—diet before and during races—deserves special treatment and will be the subject of another chapter.

While most runners now agree about correct training methods, experts still argue about the proper diet for a marathoner. Vegetarians and the advocates of animal protein-rich diets are in opposing camps. Raw-foodists of the Waerland school cite the successes of the great Swedish veteran marathoner Erik Ostbye to support their theories, while Dr. Ernest van Aaken concurs with the mainstream of sports-medicine opinion in saying that animal protein is indispensable for the runner. Students of well-known nutrition researcher Dr. Otto Brucker reject all sugar products except honey, avoid white rice and white flour, and advise the runner to obtain protein from whole grains, soy beans, and raw milk; fats from butter; and vitamins, minerals, and other nutritional elements from raw, natural sources.

At the other extreme are weight-gaining diets rich in refined carbohydrates, like those found in cake and ice cream. The standard diet for strength sports—five quarts of milk plus a half-dozen steaks—poisons the body with uric acid and a host of other toxins. Reading about such things makes you realize what a high-wire act world-class athletic competition has become.

119

While the long-distance performer does have reserves waiting to be tapped by proper diet, skepticism is well advised toward airy promises.

In case of doubt, the marathoner can rely on his own *somatic intelligence*—the term coined by German national team physician Peter Konopka to describe the unique ability of an athlete to listen to what his body is telling him.

Marathoning Is a Low-Calorie Event

Calorie consumption during the marathon is low compared with the needs of an ultramarathoner racing 100 kilometers or a bicycle road racer. Depending on his body weight, a runner will burn about 2,200 to 2,800 calories during a marathon. Sports-medicine literature generally gives higher figures. For example, a book by Josef Nocker gives the following daily consumption figures for an athlete weighing 154 pounds:

- Distance runners   minimum 4,000 calories daily, maximum 5,500
- Nordic skiers   same as for distance runners
- Swimmers   same as for distance runners
- Racing cyclists   4,000-8,000 calories
- Rowers   5,000-7,000 calories
- 6-day bicycle racers   5,000-9,000 calories
- Shotputters   4,500-6,000 calories

One thing is certain: the caloric needs of a distance runner are far below those of shotputters and bicycle racers. Though it takes 2,800 calories to run a marathon, daily training seldom calls for more than 1,000-1,500 calories. Basal metabolism requires about 1,400 calories. By adding all other daily activities, we reach a figure of about 3,500 calories, about the same required of a physical laborer. This amount calls for neither unusual amounts of food nor between-meal snacks. The energy deficit after a race is quickly filled by eating normally for a few days, while training lightly. The caloric debt from a race is paid naturally in three to four days. That "empty spot" between the hip bones (most trained marathoners don't have anything identifiable as a stomach) then disappears and the runner returns to his accustomed belt hole.

Proteins and the Marathoner

A *calorie* is the amount of heat it takes to raise the temperature of a liter of water one degree centigrade. Three kinds of food can supply caloric energy: proteins, fats, and carbohydrates. Total combustion produces 4.2 calories from one gram of carbohydrate, 9.4 calories from a gram of fat, and 4.3 calories from a gram of protein. Only carbohydrates and fats create significant caloric energy in the body, since protein is used mainly for cell repair and new-cell construction. To simplify things, carbohydrates and fats feed the fire while protein repairs the oven.

The usual figure given for daily protein requirement is one gram per each kilogram (2.2 pounds) of body weight. Children and adults who have just started getting in shape need two grams protein per kilogram of body weight. After a few weeks of exercise, when the leg muscles have adapted to exercise, a beginning runner can reduce protein intake to the 1.2- to 1.5- gram endurance-training level. The demands for strength sports are much higher. The main sources of protein are dairy products (milk, cheese, eggs) and meat. The most abundant element in everyone's diet is carbohydrate, the element needed most by runners. Sports medicine research by Heipertz shows that the relationship between carbohydrate, fat, and protein by gram weight should be 4:1:1. Nocke says the ideal level for most athletes is five grams of carbohydrate to one gram of protein to one gram of fat.

Carbohydrates are found in sugar, bread, noodles, and innumerable other foods. Carbohydrates are stored in the muscles in the form of muscle glycogen, the primary energy reserve of well-trained marathon runners. But, as you increase the distance to ultramarathons of 100 kilometers to 100 miles and beyond, running pace becomes slower and fats become increasingly important.

Energy comes from burning food with oxygen. One liter of oxygen can burn 5.04 calories of carbohydrate, but only 4.69 calories of fat. So carbohydrate is the more economical of the two. A runner notices a very definite change at the point in the marathon when his body runs out of carbohydrates and begins burning fats. This is the "wall" or "crash point"—an acute energy crisis requiring more rapid breathing while running the same speed. A study of marathon splits for world-class runners over many decades shows that the five-kilometer split between thirty-five and forty kilometers in the marathon (roughly the interval between twenty-two and twenty-five miles) was consistently two minutes slower than the first five kilometers. Children and small, lightweight women, however, seldom experience these metabolic changes because their caloric requirements are lower. Their low body weight allows them to run the entire distance without exhausting their glycogen stores.

Fat is the body's reserve energy supply. It would be a mistake to eat a fat-rich diet, though, because only "active" body fat is convertible into energy. Fatty foods taste good and satisfy, but eating them in abundance limits the body's intake of protein and carbohydrate by stilling the appetite. Fats should never make up more than 20 to 25 percent of the daily diet. They take a long time to digest and are definitely not recommended for prerace meals.

Running Faster by Fasting

Occasional days of fasting cleanse and detoxify the body and prepare the body's metabolism to meet the critical energy situation of the crash point. The ascetic eating habits of African and Japanese marathoners testify that "less is more." East Africa's kath carriers run more than 11,000 miles a year on a sparse, vegetarian diet. Dr. van Aaken frequently says that Germany's population was in excellent health during the lean years just following World War II, even though eating fewer than 2,000 calories a day. The German citizen of the 1970s suffers from all the epidemic diseases of civilization.

I do not share Dr. Nocker's view that the runner should eat a carbohydrate-rich meal after lengthy exercise. His advice that marathoners should eat 4,000 to 5,000 calories a day is inaccurate, based on other track-and-field sports. You have to train harder to get rid of these excess calories, risking injury. Many marathoners run 20 to 30 percent of their miles for the benefit of the stomach instead of to improve times. As paradoxical as this sounds, it leads many runners to develop overstress injuries.

The body seeks its own ideal weight and tries to reduce itself to the proportions of good health. The runner should try to attune himself with this natural tendency.

An injured runner can use fasting for up to a week to help maintain condition, and can then go to the starting line "untrained" but in peak form. Fasting keeps the metabolic processes in good working order. One week is too short a time for significant muscle atrophy to occur. You obviously aren't going to win any 5,000-meter track races on this method, but it helps.

Jochen Gossenberger showed the worth of fasting by abstaining from food for thirty-six hours before winning a 100-mile walk in England. Ian Jackson went beyond Dr. van Aaken's controversial fasting recommendations with 7 days of a fruit-and-vegetable-juice diet, during which he ran 130 miles. On the final day of his fast he ran twenty hilly miles in 1:55, entering a euphoric, spiritualized state, which he described beautifully in *The Runner's Diet.* * Dr. van Aaken speaks of fasting's medical benefits: liver glycogen reserves are directly available for metabolism after a thirty-six-hour fast; body weight is lowered; and blood reserves are freed from useless intestinal work during the race.

Fluid Intake

A runner loses approximately 5 percent of his body weight during a marathon and most of the loss is water. In extreme heat, losses may rise to 10 percent. Contrary to theory, in extreme heat it's not the "well-hydrated" runner but emaciated "runner types" like Abebe Bikila who have gotten through the race most economically. (See also chapter 19, "Drinking While Running.") In this chapter, we will discuss daily drinking habits, not the special requirements of racing.

We can begin by assuming that the desire to drink will be strong after a two-hour, sweat-producing run. The traditional view that you should not drink after such a run is incorrect. The body's liquid balance should be restored quickly, two quarts is not too much to drink. It's not a case of how much you drink, but of stilling natural thirst. If thirst disappears

* *The Runner's Diet, New and Revised,* by the editors of *Runner's World* (Mountain View, Calif.: World Publications, 1978).

after a bowl of soup and a pint of fluids with dinner, fine; that means the body has all it requires for the present.

After running, you should wait to drink until the stomach walls have cooled and settled down. The fluids you take should be neither too cold nor too hot. Hot tea is advisable only after races in winter, since tea increases perspiration and electrolyte losses.

Water. The runner who has a nearby source of fresh spring water containing natural minerals is fortunate indeed. One of the great delights of training in the mountains is stopping for water at a crystal-clear stream. Bottle mineral water is not recommended because of the carbonation, but you can remove the bubbles by adding a pinch of salt to the bottle. Valuable natural substances are removed from mineral water in the bottling process, and the added gas does nothing but bloat the runner's stomach.

Tea. Black tea with honey and salt is an excellent postrace drink for the marathoner. The standard drink at marathon finish lines was formerly black tea with dextrose (glucose), but it increased thirst and made blood-sugar levels soar before plummeting into reactive hypoglycemia. Concentrated glucose irritates the stomach membrane and often leads to emergency rejection of the already-acidified contents of the stomach by vomiting.

Honey is better than sugar, but only in small quantities. Tea contains a caffeinelike substance called *thein,* which is either stimulating or relaxing, depending on how the tea is brewed. To make a stimulating tea, let it brew for three to four minutes; for a sedative tea, let it brew longer, up to ten minutes. Longer brewing brings out the tannic acid, increasing the bitter taste, which can be disguised with honey. In this way you can precisely control the effect of tea.

If black tea doesn't agree with you, you may want to try hibiscus-blossom tea, which some runners have found agreeable when served hot in cold weather and cold in hot weather. Hibiscus Camomile tea is suggested for sensitive stomachs.

Beer. Many runners enjoy beer after a race or workout, and they seem to be able to drink large quantities without harm.

(Near beer, containing no alcohol, is a favorite of some runners.) Runners such as Lutz Philipp (sub-2:20) and Gunther Mielke ignore the outcries of purists while guzzling their finish-line brew. I discovered the virtues of beer as a postrun drink long ago. I was totally exhausted at the end of a race, had a raging thirst, and grabbed the first thing someone handed me in a bottle. I promptly threw up. For the next several hours I threw up everything I ate or drank, until finally I tried a few bread crumbs with a swallow of beer. It stayed down. From then on I've avoided all the sweetened drinks that made my stomach do flip-flops and have headed straight for the nearest beer.

Beer drinking has great value for various endurance exercises, except for long-distance skiing in cold weather. The alcohol in beer (normally up to 5 percent) has a sedative effect matching that of the hops. (Near beer has the hops without the alcohol.) Since beer comes from biological rather than mineral sources, it contains a number of useful substances that are not found in tea. A quart of beer supplies about 450 calories, which help to replenish depleted energy reserves quickly. A quart of beer has about the same amount of carbohydrate as a quarter-pound of bread, but goes down faster and is metabolized more quickly. The B-complex vitamins are strongly represented in beer, especially vitamin B_2 (nearly the minimum daily requirement in a quart). Brewer's yeast, incidentally, is the natural food containing the highest content of B vitamins.

I am not advocating alcoholism. But what's the good of suffering on occasion from nausea, nutritional deficiency symptoms, and insomnia, if all these ills can be removed simply and efficiently? When Frank Shorter was in Munich for the 1972 Olympic Games, he attended a small social gathering just after his marathon win. Shorter was emphatic in his praise of Bavarian beer; it seems to have agreed with him, and he certainly earned it.

Bouillon Broth. A salty beef or chicken broth meets the body's need to restore its salt balance naturally.

Coca Cola. Some world-class runners drink a cold bottle of Coke immediately after a run. Coca Cola is mostly foam by the time it reaches the stomach, so its effects on the stomach walls

TABLE 9

Energy Needs of a 2:20 Marathoner

Weight (kg).	Calories Required	Calories Per km.	Total Glycogen Required (g.)
54.5	2,180	51.6	544
59.0	2,365	56.1	592
63.5	2,530	60.0	632
68.0	2,710	64.3	678
72.5	2,880	68.3	720
77.0	3,065	72.6	766
81.5	3,230	76.6	808
86.0	3,415	80.9	853
91.0	3,584	84.9	896
95.0	3,766	89.2	941
100.0	3,933	93.2	983

TABLE 10

Calorie Needs of A Marathoner

Body Weight (kg.)	Finish Time (hours)		Calories (kcal.)
	2:20	=	2,180
54.5	2:37	=	2,166
	2:54	=	2,105
	2:20	=	2,884
72.5	2:37	=	2,842
	2:54	=	2,801
	2:20	=	2,933
100.0	2:37	=	3,877
	2:54	=	2,897

are diminished and it may refresh without the shock effect of other sweetened drinks. The stimulating substances in Coke work against the usual severe drop in blood pressure that immediately follow a race and help the runner get through states of psychological apathy. The sweetness does seem more tolerable than that of other drinks.

Other Drinks. After hard exercise you should avoid milk, cocoa, coffee, wine, lemonade, sparkling water, and tap water. Never mind that milk is man's native drink; cow's milk is poorly handled by the digestive tracts of many runners. Other foods that may cause allergic reactions and should be suspected in cases of digestive upset are: legumes (peas, lentils, peanuts, etc.), onions, pork, chocolate, strawberries, and lemons. *Runner's World* medical editor Dr. George Sheehan reported the case of a marathon runner who was allergic to the gluten in wheat and experienced severe diarrhea after eating bread, though this only happened during long runs. The runner was helped by switching to rice as a staple grain.

The highly trained body of a marathoner has about 500 grams of glycogen in reserve, according to Dr. John Brotherhood. Brotherhood says that an all-out marathon requires 650 grams of glycogen. The difference comes from either metabolizing fat or from high-carbohydrate mid-race intake. The following table shows that lightweight runners of both sexes have an advantage, and thus do not need to consume carbohydrates during the race. Brotherhood's figure of 650 grams applies to runners weighing more than 143 pounds. From the standpoint of energy metabolism, it's just not possible to propel a heavy body through the marathon distance at 2:20 pace. The heavier runner thus needs to eat a carbohydrate-rich diet and to take nutritional substances during the race.

Chapter 17

Carbohydrate-Loading

In the late sixties and early seventies a special diet plan was devised in the English-speaking countries for the last weeks before a marathon race. This plan, called *carbohydrate-loading,* made its way through the ranks of western world-class marathon runners like a plague.

English chemist Dr. Ron Hill, one of the first runners of his class to adopt this diet successfully, used it to become 1969 European marathon champion. He caught and passed Belgium's Gaston Roelants in the final miles of the classic marathon course from Marathon to Athens. In the following non-Olympic years he was considered the best marathoner in the world, with a Commonwealth Games win in 1970 and a record-breaking victory at Boston in 1970. Hill, a tinkerer who designed his own running clothes—including the reflective outfit he wore at the Munich Games—was the figurehead for the new dietary method.

According to Swedish researcher Saltin, the body's muscle glycogen can be increased significantly by eating slmost exclusively carbohydrates for three days. The working muscle produces energy from glycogen and fat. When, as happens in a marathon race, 80 percent of the body's maximal oxygen uptake level is exceeded, the body reaches into its carbohydrate reserves for fuel. When this reserve is exhausted, the body switches over to fats for energy metabolism. This metabolic switchover, drastic in its effects, is the infamous crash point or "wall" at twenty miles. Saltin's theory proved correct in practice. After three days of concentrated carbohydrate intake, cross-country ski racers, racing cyclists, and long-distance runners all improved their performances. Glycogen levels rose in both muscles and liver. Fuel reserves lasted longer, leading in theory to a positive jump in performance. In time an exact ritual for carbohydrate-loading was developed with several phases.

Phase One. A week before the race, run a time trial of about twenty-five miles at 75 percent of race pace, or else an all-out six-mile run.

Phase Two. Six days before the race—that is, immediately following the time trial—begin 3 days of low-carbohydrate diet. In this period, eat only proteins and fats, as far as this is possible. The list of permissible foods during this period includes beef, pork, sausage, fish, eggs, cheese, butter, milk, yogurt, cream, pudding, vegetable oils, margarine, mushrooms, asparagus, chocolate, cocoa, and nuts—all in unlimited quantities. Since they contain carbohydrates, you can eat small quantities of the following: green beans, cabbage, cauliflower, spinach, celery, pumpkin (all cooked), endive salad, green salad, watercress salad, tomato salad, rhubarb, gooseberries, lemon, grapefruit, and olives. Sugars are forbidden, and no sweetened or starch-containing drinks should be used. Drink only small amounts of milk. During this phase the quantity of food eaten should not be increased, and the carbohydrate intake must be reduced to a minimum.

CARBOHYDRATE-RICH FOODS

	Weight (Grams)	Calories	Protein (Grams)	Carbo-hydrate (Grams)
Corn Products				
Cornflakes	28	109	2.2	24.2
Fresh Corn	140	71	2.6	16.4
Cornmeal	114	403	10.4	83.6
Grain Products				
White Bread	23	62	2.0	11.6
Rye Bread	23	56	2.1	11.9
Cracked Wheat	23	60	2.0	11.9
French Bread	20	58	1.8	11.1
Saltine Cracker	28	123	2.6	20.3

	Weight	Calories	Protein	Carbo.
Candies				
Milk Chocolate	28	147	2.2	16.1
Choc. Fudge	28	113	.8	21.3
Plain Caramel	28	113	1.1	21.7
Jelly Beans	28	104	tr	26.4
Butterscotch	28	112	tr	26.9
Marshmallows	28	90	.6	22.8
Jams & Jellies				
Jellies	20	55	tr	14.3
Jams	20	54	.1	14.0
Sugars				
White, Granulated	195	75	0	194.0
Honey	21	64	tr	17.3
Brown	14	52	0	13.5
Powdered Confectioners	8	31	0	8.0
Desserts				
Cake, Chocolate, with Icing	114	394	3.9	75.9
Cake, Devil's Food	114	386	5.0	66.5
Chocolate Chip Cookies	28	134	1.5	19.8
Oatmeal-Raisin Cookies	28	123	1.8	20.8
Canned Fruits				
Fruit Cocktail	227	173	0.9	44.7
Peaches in Syrup	253	197	1.0	50.9
Pears in Syrup	230	175	0.5	45.1
Pineapple in Syrup	262	194	0.8	50.8
Dried Fruit				
Apples	260	202	0.8	52.5
Apricots	285	242	4.6	65.2
Peaches	114	297	3.5	77.5
Prunes	258	307	2.6	81.0
Fruit Juices				
Orange, Fresh	185	87	1.3	20.2
Grapefruit	185	72	0.9	16.9
Grape	185	122	0.4	30.7
Prune	192	148	0.8	36.5
Cranberry	188	122	tr	31.0
Vegetable Juices and Sauces				
Tomato	181	38	1.3	48.0
Catsup	17	18	0.3	23.6
Vegetable Cocktail	181	31	1.6	6.5
Vegetables				
Potato	100	93	2.6	21.1
Winter Squash	205	113	3.9	28.7
Peas	138	116	8.7	19.9
Lima Beans	170	189	12.9	33.7

Normal training is continued through the low-carbohydrate period. In this way muscle glycogen is almost totally depleted. Muscle glycogen levels will decline in four or five days from 1.5 percent to 0.9 percent. During this time the runner will feel completely limp—not just while running, but all day long. Even staunch advocates of the diet, like England's Dr. Brotherhood, advise eating a little glycogen to relieve nausea and headache. Another result of the protein diet will be a two to five-pound weight loss.

Phase Three. An abrupt change is made in the high-carbohydrate diet at the end of the first period. In this phase the cells become unusually "hungry" for glycogen. Dr. Brotherhood says, "This procedure leads to a rapid increase in glycogen which exceeds the original levels by a factor of 4 to 4.5 percent. It seems the muscles accumulate a substance during the deficiency phase which allows them to store much more glycogen. It has likewise been shown that liver glycogen reacts in the same manner."

At this stage the menu takes on a completely new look. The following foods are recommended: cake, white bread, rice, rolled oats, ice cream, etc. Meat and other protein- and fat-rich foods should be avoided since they displace carbohydrates in the stomach. The runner should drink sweetened drinks up to an hour before the race—especially if it's a warm day—in order to go into the race fully hydrated and with a high blood-sugar level.

It is quite obvious, however, that the athlete who eats only carbohydrates will gain weight rapidly. When glycogen is stored, it binds to the body 2½ times its weight in water. The marathon runner whose weight has remained constant for months may now be subjected to stressful up-and-down fluctuations during the important prerace phase. He can gain six or seven pounds while carbohydrate-loading, and as a result may feel heavy and stiff. Even those who advocate the extreme seven-day version of the plan say a marathon runner should cut back on his food intake when he reaches three pounds over his average weight. Unlimited weight gains are less important only for the 100-kilometer race.

Cierpinski and Shorter

Immediately after the Montreal Olympic marathon I asked gold medalist Waldemar Cierpinski and silver medalist Frank Shorter whether they had used the Saltin diet. Each said no. It is known, though, that Shorter has tried it on occasion, including just before his 1972 victory at Munich.

I tried carbohydrate-loading in 1971 and ran 2:20. I cannot say now whether it was actually a help or a hindrance. I later stopped using the diet.

Theoretical discussion regarding the Saltin diet is still in progress. Dr. van Aaken, who recommends fasting before a marathon, rejects carbohydrate-loading completely. He believes it is unrealistic to talk of strictly separate fat and carbohydrate metabolisms during exercise. According to van Aaken, the body uses both sources of energy at all times while running; it is only the proportions that change after twenty miles. In the January 1975 issue of *Spiridon* magazine he wrote: "Carbohydrate is merely the small change of energy reserves. Much more important are the great energy reserves of fat." He distinguished between active fat and passive, or stored, fat. The percentage of active fat is especially high in women. On the basis of standard calorie calculations the glycogen reserves of the body will never be sufficient for a marathon run. In fact, ultramarathon races at a pace of 50 to 70 percent of maximal oxygen uptake are not run on the "small change" of glycogen but with the "big bills" of fat, specifically the free fatty acids. (See also chapter 25 on the 100-kilometer run.)

My feeling—as a medical layman and as an experienced marathon runner—is that the whole discussion is too theoretical. For example, when Gunther Mielke surveyed world-class runners regarding their use of the Saltin diet, he found that most runners consider the procedure completely out of the question for hot-weather racing. It was, in a gruesomely literal sense, a flash in the pan: the concentrated carbohydrate intake led to problems in the gastrointestinal tract. Dr. George Sheehan likewise warns of a number of cases of dysentery resulting from use of the Saltin diet. For example, it is not recommended for the older runner. And it is still a matter of debate just how often carbo-loading can be used with success. Sudden energy collapse, side stitches, diarrhea, poor mental concentration, and impaired tactical judgment are all potential symptoms of switching one's diet drastically within just a few days.

I think, however, that we must make a distinction between types of carbohydrates. Concentrates like glucose pills, ice cream, and cake give the body's metabolism, including the gastrointestinal tract, a more massive challenge than do foods such as rolled oats. Grains, taken in the form of granola and sweetened with honey instead of refined sugar, are recommended for enriching the diet while filling the body's carbohydrate depots during the last days before a marathon. You should not change the emphasis of your diet radically from your normal, everyday diet. My experience has been that tinkering with diet just before a race often does more harm than good.

One thing above all: because training mileage is cut back in the days before a marathon, the runner's food and drink should be restricted in accordance with the body's reduced needs. The idea that a runner should go to the start with plenty of liquids inside him and a high blood-sugar level is highly controversial. Research findings on this topic are extremely varied. Does blood sugar rise when you eat concentrated glucose before a race or does it turn around and fall drastically because of the manner in which concentrated sugars affect insulin levels? Researchers are still looking for a more precise answer. Recent American findings contradict once established truths, and confirm the instinct-based procedure of longtime racers in avoiding sweets before running. Runners from the African desert often drink large amounts of cool water in the early morning and plenty of strong, sweetened tea after running all day, but none in between.

In discussions of carbohydrate diet, a marathoner's calorie demands are often assumed to be fixed, but they are not. Studies in New York have shown that marathon runners (up to 120 pounds) have no need of carbohydrate-loading: Such marathoners run well on their bodies' stored glycogen—especially women and children. If you weigh less than 143 pounds you can avoid time losses in marathons by training your body to make the transition from carbohydrate to fat metabolism after twenty miles. The body has in storage about 650 grams of glycogen, which will be used for the race. If you weigh more than 143 pounds, you will need to increase your glycogen supply either by the Saltin diet or by taking drinks during the race.

Modified Carbo-Loading Diet

The Saltin diet has a partial placebo effect, causing the runner to believe in its effectiveness. If you weaken this faith, the magic vanishes. A runner who's several pounds heavier after carbohydrate-loading may require the extra glycogen he's painfully added just to get his extra weight through the 26 miles. He'll surely lose every possible advantage if, at 21 miles, he's forced into the bushes with an attack of diarrhea.

The Saltin diet does show, however, that a runner's diet may be altered beneficially during the light-training phase before a race, as long as this is done in moderation. I do recommend the all-out run 7 to 8 days before the race. But instead of the forced, and unaccustomed, high-protein phase, the runner should fast for a day after the hard workout, with just a light breakfast and then water for the rest of the day. Follow this with two days of normal eating, taking care not to overeat the day after the fast, which would neutralize its beneficial effects. During the last three days, emphasize carbohydrates: rolled oats and wheat germ, dried fruit, yogurt for breakfast, and boiled brown rice with vegetables. Two hours before the race I recommend eating one of those terrible-tasting astronaut meals that come in a bag or can and contain all the essential nutritional elements, especially free fats and electrolytes.

Chapter 18

Electrolytes and Vitamins

We know today that the role of vitamins in sports has long been overrated, and that the need for electrolytes in long-lasting physical exercise is vital. Electrolytes and vitamins make up the mortar that hold together the building blocks of good diet. Electrolytes are substances that carry electrical currents, and serve in conduction of neural impulses in the nervous system. Electrolyte deficiencies cause cramps in the calves and upper thighs, mental disturbances, and even complete failure of the circulatory system. Many a collapse could have been prevented by keeping the body's mineral household in order.

The important electrolytes are sodium chloride (table salt), potassium, various phosphates, calcium, and magnesium. The marathoner loses all these in sweat while running. The blood can flow normally when deficient in salt, but this is a rare deficiency even in hot weather. A more common problem is overacidification of the muscles from sodium deficiency. Rising acid levels, combined with simultaneous increases in lactic acid in the muscle, are signs of too little sodium, which helps maintain alkaline levels in the muscles.

"Why do marathoners spice their food so heavily?" I was once asked by the waiter in my favorite restaurant. The answer is quite simply that we replenish our salt losses while eating. (Note that we're talking about sodium here, as contained in table salt.) Meanwhile, it has been proven that though salt is an essential electrolyte, marathoners rarely have deficiencies in sodium chloride. It's more important to take other electrolytes on a regular, preventive basis, especially potassium, phosphates, and magnesium.

Things now get complicated because there are two divergent opinions on this subject. One states we should eat lots of salt to bind water in the body, supplying liquids for sweat loss and preventing salt deficiency. According to this view, proper regulation of the body's water balance can stimulate the kidneys and adrenal glands. The other opinion holds that a marathoner should consume little salt, thus preventing retention of unnecessary water with its added weight, as well as delaying the onset of perspiration. It is known that the runner eats a lot of salt will sweat it out again in large quantities. This in itself is not bad, but sweat losses stimulated by eating too much salt also wash out other more important minerals.

The opposing views here represent carefully planned eating on one hand, and a kind of ascetic "naturalism" on the other. I've had success with a mixed, middle-of-the-road procedure. While training, especially during high-stress phases, I eat a salt-rich diet; just before a race when training lightly, I eat low-salt meals. The motto here is "be able to sweat, but start sweating as late as possible when racing."

Commercial Drinks

As I said earlier, salt is not the most important mineral. In the last few years a number of drinks and powders have become established on the market by promising scientifically balanced electrolyte replacement formulas. The best known of these in Germany is the Fitogen pill, which contains 217 milligrams (mg.) of sodium dihydrogen phosphate, 160 mg. of sodium monohydrogen phosphate, 150 mg. of sodium chloride and 20.2 mg. of potassium bicarbonate. I've had the best experiences with Fitogen of all the preparations I've tried, taking it both on a preventive basis and after races. In cool weather one tablet with breakfast seems to be enough. Recovery time for my leg muscles has been shortened considerably. Instead of five or six days of muscle soreness and heavy legs after a marathon, this condition disappears in about three days. Without Fitogen I could never have won a 5,000-meter race with a final sprint, just six days after running a 2:16:45 marathon.

For all my enthusiasm, I advise the runner to take this preparation sparingly, not to use it on a regular basis, but to take the recommended high dosage of three to four tablets only in very hot weather. In mild or cool weather one tablet before a marathon and two afterward is enough, as is one tablet after hard training.

Electrolyte drinks are becoming increasingly popular. In the United States they've been used widely since 1967, in West Germany since 1972. The best-known drinks in the U.S. are Gatorade, Body Punch, and ERG (also called Gookinaid). In Germany, the most popular drink is Champ, and in Switzerland it is Beneroc-Roche. Gatorade, which is offered to the runner at every street corner during the Boston Marathon, is too sweet. This is an example of the persisting belief that calorie-replacement is the most important thing. Gatorade also has too little potassium. Champ, the German drink, contains four parts sodium, two parts potassium, and one part magnesium. The magnesium, absent in Fitogen, is especially valuable. But in my opinion the sugar content of Champ (in the form of saccharides) is still too high. Beneroc has a balanced composition. The ingredients of the American drink ERG, on the other hand, are kept strictly secret.

I've had the best luck with ERG, concocted by California marathoner and chemist Bill Gookin. Gookin developed the drink after analyzing his own sweat losses, and comparing them with those of other runners. The sugar content is relatively low, and ERG contains no magnesium. Gookin made the drink known via his own successes as a veteran runner.

One thing should not be forgotten. There is more potassium in one glass of beer than in a whole pitcher of Gatorade, the analysis of which is known. The runner who drinks should also realize that tests reveal the stomach can absorb only 0.8 liters of liquid per hour during physical exercise. This means that more than three cups of any drink every three miles will be useless.

The role of magnesium, which has an alkaline function in the body similar to potassium, is frequently underestimated. It appears in very concentrated form in spinach, and potassium losses during a marathon are very high, as Dr. Kenneth Cooper discovered in tests at the 1969 Boston race. The rage for magnesium came to an abrupt halt, though, when it was discovered that too much just before a race can cause diarrhea. There is magnesium in Champ. If you take another brand of drink or tablet before the race, take a magnesium pill along with it.

The oldest marathon-nutrition tip I know of also involves the quickly-eliminated metal, magnesium. Before World War II, experienced marathoners carried a dried plum in a pocket to stop hunger pangs during the race. This habit, which I learned from former German national coach and national marathon champion Ernst Weber of Berlin, seemed to involve placebo effects operating through the chewing muscles and stomach glands. Today we know that dried plums are very high in magnesium.

Iron is also considered an electrolyte, but it is discussed in detail in the chapter on women runners.

Vitamin deficiencies due to overprocessing and overcooking modern canned and packaged foods have been alleviated in recent years by a relative excess of vitamins. Even the most poorly bottled lemonade drinks boast of their vitamin C content. Vitamin C plays a certain role in the prevention of colds. For a while, vitamin E was surrounded by myths related to increased sexual potency, which accounted for temporary out-of-stock conditions at drugstores. However, this promise was not fulfilled. Vitamins C and E are important for the marathon runner. The former can be taken in dosages of up to 500 mg. per day; higher doses are eliminated in the urine. Vitamin E has an extraordinarily positive effect on the muscles during endurance exercise and has been given in high dosages to East German athletes for many years. Ludwig Prokop found that the requirement for an endurance athlete is five times greater than for the average person, while the athlete's requirement for vitamin C is about three times greater than normal. A generally higher overall vitamin need exists for the runner. During the recovery phase, the entire vitamin B complex is important, especially vitamin B-2, which plays a role in the enzyme systems, and vitamin B-12, which affects oxygen transport in the blood.

Chapter 19

Drinking While Running

Another hotly disputed question is: how can a marathon runner deal with water losses during a race? During a 26-mile run the body loses 5 to 10 percent of its fluids, which has led experts to question whether runners should drink while racing or go thirsty. Body water is always lost while racing, and the "abstainers" say drinking only stimulates the body to sweat harder and cause it to lose valuable electrolytes. The prevailing opinion now suggests runners should fully hydrate the body and take preventive measure in hot weather and keep water losses to a minimum during races by drinking at regular intervals. This view is especially strong in the English-speaking countries. countries.

In Germany, Professor Harald Mellerowicz of Berlin advocates heavy fluid intake before and during the race. His original dosages, in liters, were simply impractical. In addition, muscle-biopsy studies in Muncie, Indiana showed that he leaned too heavily on high-dextrose drinks that are poorly absorbed by sensitive digestive membranes and have no purposeful effect. After taking these drinks it was twelve hours before glycogen levels rose in the muscles; thus the drinks are completely ineffectual during a race. Practice showed this long ago, causing runners to switch their attention from dextrose to electrolytes. Mellerowicz and various Anglo-Saxon researchers measured the stresses on the body during long road races. Mellerowicz made a study in Ulcinj in southern Yugoslavia that compared runners who consumed fluids with those who did not, and found the drinking runners recovered faster after the race and showed lower rectal body temperatures. Some well-trained nondrinking runners had body temperatures between 106 and 107.6 degrees, which is symptomatic of near-delirium. Body temperatures of the drinkers were lower. Unfortunately, Mellerowicz made a serious error in the method used in his tests. He did not simulate racing conditions, and allowed the nondrinking control group to stand and watch the other runners while they drank, before everyone started running again. This was completely unrealistic. For one thing, in races runners normally lose time drinking at the aid stations, and therefore face the stress of making up lost ground. This hinders them in their drinking. On the other hand, abstinence from drinking was not rewarded as it would have been in an actual race, since runners did not gain a single inch for their "tactic." It's no wonder the drinkers came out the physiological victors in such a lame test.

Most marathoners feel the problem is not to get over the course as safely as possible, but to run as fast as they can. At least, this is the way many runners think. For the runner who wants to spare himself, drinking is recommended. But for the runner who wants to win, or who is fighting for every half-minute under 2:40, other concepts apply. What does the regular drinker gain if he arrives at the finish line fresh, but loses to someone who finishes five minutes earlier totally exhausted, not having wasted time and energy along the way? We already gave the example of the successful auto racing driver who coasted through the finish line with a near-empty gas tank.

Dr. van Aaken suggested that Mellerowicz and other researchers made a further error in concept: that digestion of drinks consumed during a race pulls blood out of the peripheral muscles to the stomach and intestines. This leads to an energy deficit for the oxygen transport systems.

The thirsty runner has advantages resembling those of the fasting runner. He avoids distracting chores at drink stations and he does not subject himself to the danger of electrolyte losses through sweating, which are provoked by drinking liquids. The nondrinking runner's clear disadvantage is that he finishes feeling worse. As long as there are no preliminary heats in the marathon and it's winner-take-all, the runner may be able to put up with this inconvenience. It is equally strange that the percentage of body water lost is lowest in runners who start the race relatively dry. Abebe Bikila never took drinks during a race. Through proper training I was able to run the hot, high-altitude marathon at the 1968 Olympics in Mexico City (83 degrees at 7,600 feet altitude) without consuming a single drop all the way.

Let's call an end to theoretical discussion. Wet or dry, the main thing is to get through the marathon distance. I would advise all beginning and first-year marathoners to drink during races. The same is true of anyone who has felt a great need to drink during training. In addition, runners with relatively poor endurance or who weigh more than 154 pounds should also drink. Special circumstances may force the nondrinker over to the aid-station table. This is the case in great heat, where temperature is actually less important than high relative humidity and in cold weather, as in half-marathons in the winter.

In all these cases the runner should be prepared to take liquids during the race. Since drinking habits can add or subtract minutes to a performance, the runner should know well in advance what he's going to drink, where the drink stations are, and at which ones he'll stop. It is best of all to have a helper place drink bottles at the aid tables. These should contain one's own made-to-order brew or a commercial drink that has proved tolerable. This way the runner will be certain of not being handed a much-too-hot cup of tea or an ice-cold cup of Kool-aid. Hot drinks add heat to an already overheated body; even in cold weather, they have been shown to hinder rather han help the runner. Hot drinks can be taken only in small gulps, and not at all while running at race pace. Cold drinks irritate the stomach lining and can lead to nausea and side stitch.

Having private bottles at the aid stations is most important if the runner wants to get over the course in a fast time. It's a good idea to practice picking a plastic bottle off a table without stopping, throwing the head back and squirting the contents down as fast as possible. Friedel Wiggershaus, a master of the art, barely missed making the 1978 German Olympic team. Despite my tactic of using drink stops to accelerate and break contact with opponents, I was never able to gain more than a meter on Friedel. On a muggy June day on the lower Rhein he sprinted faster than me for a cold jug of water that was beckoning from an aid table, and then splashed it over his head without even changing his step rate. I was nonplussed. My radiator was still dry and, thoroughly deflated by this scene, I lost more than a half-minute to Friedel before reaching the finish line.

It is enormously important, not only to drink fast and maintain speed, but to drink without filling your stomach with bubbles. The latter can cause nausea, a bloated feeling, and stitches.

America's Gayle Barron, who ran a 2:47:43.2 for third place at the world women's marathon in October 1976, is a slow drinker. Gayle, a dark-haired beauty from Atlanta, Georgia, drank at every aid station and finished the race with enormous reserves. At every drink table she stopped dead, looked over the offering of cups and fruits, took a little of this and a little of that, and then chased off to make up the twenty to thirty yards she had lost. Gayle's sprinting wasted more energy than she could possibly have gained by drinking, and in this manner surely gave away second place to Kim Merritt, who finished in 2:47:11.2. When I mentioned this to Gayle after the race, she realized her error. She told me she had simply done what she had seen the American men in her time category do in mixed races. I pointed out that a man racing in the 2:50 class wasn't too worried about gaining or losing a minute or so, but that a woman of her class could gain several places in world lists by making her drinking procedure more efficient.

We have proceeded on the assumption that the runner will supply his own plastic bottles. On the bottles he should write in large, clear letters his name and the mileage of the respective drink station. Use a marking pen and write something like "Jerome Drayton, 25 miles." The majority of runners, of course, just help themselves from the cups on the tables. If you're among them, save yourself a little time by finding out in advance what kind of drinks will be available and where the stations will be located. Some race organizers use signs to indicate water, tea, ERG, and so on. Where this highly recommended service is missing, the runner will have to look out for himself, since you can't look through a paper cup and see what's in it.

Those little paper cups for tea or water have the fatal flaw of being wider at the top than at the bottom. While this may be helpful for Joe Consumer guzzling on a barstool, for the marathoner it is just plain poor design. Grab a paper cup delicately from the bottom between thumb and forefinger and sweep it up toward your thirsty mouth. It will invariably arrive crushed flat and half-empty. The other half of the liquid will pleasantly cool your chest. But if it is sweetened tea it will begin to smell bad within the next two miles and you won't be able to run away from the odor. I recommend the following unconventional grip for the person drinking on the run. Place the palm of your hand over the top of the cup and hold onto the sides with your fingers. You won't spill a drop and there will be a small opening between the thumb and index finger, allowing you to appease your thirst in a more or less controlled fashion. It sounds pretty simple, but it takes practice. This method does not work with hot tea (which you shouldn't pick anyway), because you'll burn your hand after lifting the cup.

Of all the usual drinks, you should be most suspicious of tea. First take a small sip and see how sweet it is, rather than gulping it down and later having it rejected by the stomach. Sometimes the tea is brewed in different kitchens, and varies from one table to the next. Be cautious, not only with tea but with lemons as well. Emil Zatopek said after his Olympic marathon victory that he'd passed the lead runner in the race in large part because the fellow had taken a bit of a lemon at an aid station. Zatopek said his confidence increased enormously when he saw this. Zatopek was well acquainted with physiology and knew that a body already overacidified by racing at high speeds would react allergically to sour fruit. Lemons are nonetheless common at many long road races, due to the race organizers' leanings toward vitamin C.

Happily, nobody's come up with the idea of providing little cups of milk for protein during a race. Churned by the movements of running, it would turn to cheese, causing severe stomach pain, if not diarrhea.

Oranges, available at nearly all aid stations, have a fairly high acid content. Dilute grapefruit juice or the blueberries served at Scandinavian ski marathons would be better. If you can't deal with feelings of hunger during a race, eat a banana and chew it carefully. Bananas are easily digested. They contain potassium, and their natural fruit sugars do not disturb the stomach or metabolic processes as severely as concentrated glucose.

I would like to warn the runner even more strongly against

drinking water during a race than I did about lemons. Pure spring water would be fine, but it is difficult to find water without additives. Water has generally been somewhat contaminated before it reaches the aid stations.

Even worse than drinking from dirty water tanks is the custom of sucking on sponges which—the devil only knows—could have been lying in a puddle on the ground just minutes before, thrown there by another runner. Drinking from sponges of unknown ancestry is both undisciplined and irresponsible. It would be ideal to be handed one's own sponge, dipped in one's own drink by one's own personal handler at a time when one needs it, but racing rules forbid this—a technicality that is generally overlooked in hot-weather races of a noninternational character.

At the 1974 world veterans' championships in Paris there were, indeed, excesses. Totally dehydrated runners were on their bellies sipping from puddles because the aid stations had run out of water. In my opinion, though, one of the virtues of the marathon runner is to run not just against the opponent or the clock, but against his own weaknesses and physical needs. This is not true of runners with weak kidneys.

Taking liquids during a race will only be effective if done in orderly fashion. In normal weather this means having your first drink as late as possible in the race, skipping some drink stops rather than filling the body with fluids it doesn't really need. Only in extremely hot weather, where the runner should think twice about entering a marathon in the first place, should he begin drinking as soon as possible. The fear of having to stop in the bushes because of drinking too much is unfounded, because the body's own fluid requirements will be so high that the kidneys will scarcely have any work to do at all.

Chapter 20

Cooling Down

The marathon runner needs appropriate cooling methods to help prevent heat-accumulation. Burning calories while running 26 miles creates internal heat that the body cannot eliminate beyond a certain point. The result is a fever caused by the accumulation of uneliminated heat.

How do we treat our patient—the marathoner past mile 20—who has a fever? Give him fluids, and since medication is out of the question, also try lowering his temperature by external methods. Cool his wrists, forehead, neck and shoulders; apply ice cubes against the skin; and frequently bathe his body in cool water. All these treatments for the marathon runner are more important than drinking fluids. In air temperatures exceeding 68 degrees F the runner should stop at every aid station after he begins perspiring and pour water on himself for external cooling.

The most effective coolant is a sponge. You can do many useful things with a sponge full of water. I've developed a kind of ritual with the sponge that has worked well for me. First I wipe my forehead and cheeks, and then shoulders, squeezing a little so the water runs down my back. Then I wet my neck and squeeze the sponge over my chest, and then let the water drip on both thighs and wipe the backs of the knees. After wetting each wrist over the pulse, I squeeze all the remaining water onto my feet so my shoes will be wet for awhile. This takes just a few seconds and doesn't alter my running style. The biggest problem is getting a full sponge.

It is most important to keep your head cool. In extreme

151

temperatures I've always poured water over my head. The runner should not shy from giving himself a complete shower with a hose or bucket to prevent heat accumulation. The shock may bring him momentarily out of rhythm, but it's not dangerous. The runner, unlike the swimmer, is protected from severe reactions by his own perspiration. It is much easier for the body to handle several complete drenchings than to keep running in a fully dehydrated state. In extreme heat, the last quarter of the race should be run sponge in hand or with a wet handkerchief tied loosely around the neck. Many runners stick their heads into a bucket of water before beginning the race to keep heat down to a minimum from the start.

In the Tour de France bicycle race, fights are not uncommon at water stops, where the riders even leave their bicycles to get cooled off. In my hottest marathon race, the 1971 German championships where the thermometer held steady at 86 degrees and the humidity was nearly unbearable, I had the good fortune to be handled by former world professional cycling champion Rudi Altig. (The crowds were cheering louder for him than for the runners.) When the water at the aid stations became too warm, Altig collected a huge pile of ice. He just walked up and knocked on farmhouse doors, collecting ice cubes from freezers and refrigerators. It was pure balsam on my wounds! Let it be mentioned—and remembered at appropriate moments—that out of fairness I sent Altig back with ice and a wet sponge to Hans Hellbach, who was following me. I finished second and qualified for the European championships race. But four weeks later at Helsinki both Lutz Philipp, the current German marathon titlist, and I were still suffering so badly from the aftereffects of the previous hot-weather race that we failed to run in top form.

Such cases prove that the old limitations on drinking prescribed by international rules—and as followed in 1976 at Montreal—are totally senseless and dangerous to one's health. On the recommendation of the international organization of sports physicians, the limitations have been dropped. Marathons should in no case be held in temperatures exceeding 77 degrees.

Cooling is helpful not only in hot weather. The fastest races are usually run in conditions that reporters later describe as "unfavorable cool weather with light winds and light rain, which surprisingly produced a number of exceptional performances." Aside from the fact that world-class runners experience less friction on wet pavement, rain provides continuous cooling that prevents internal temperatures from rising. Rain also washes off accumulations of salt and sweat, thus clearing the pores. And wind, which makes for slower times in all races, may have a positive, cooling effect if it comes from the front with moderate force. A soft opposing wind may be much more pleasant than a following wind on a warm day, since an opposing wind cools the runner even more. Good times are even run in winter marathons.

Part Four

Sophisticated Marathon Training

1978 BOSTON MARATHON
5
TIGER SHOES
NEW ZEALAND
1978 BOSTON MA
1
1978 BOSTON MA
3
TIGER SHO

Chapter 21

Marathoning Tactics

Consistent pace is, of course, the first commandment of marathoning. A runner who's sensitive to pacing and rhythm will maintain consistent speed if he can match his condition on race day to a set of well-planned split times. Nevertheless, other tactics add excitement to the sport. Tactics will always be important, whether your goal is an age-group trophy, first place, or just outfoxing an old running buddy. The tactical variations in the marathon are as numerous as they are in the half-mile. It wouldn't be possible to detail all the possible tactics here. Some have been discussed in different chapters, such as kicking hard through aid stations to break away from the group you're in.

Before diving into specific tactics, here's a tactical tip, borrowed from *Runner's World* magazine, that can win you valuable yards right at the starting line. One minute before the gun goes off, yell very loudly, "Oh my God, I dropped my contact lens?" Get down on your knees in a racing crouch. When the gun goes off, and everyone else has his nose buried in the pavement, you're off . . . valuable seconds ahead of the pack.

The Front-Runner

The above bit of underhandedness favors only the front-runner, or pace-setter. The front-runner moves into the lead early in the race, if not right from the gun; if he's successful, he'll maintain a lead all the way to the finish. It takes both great courage and a well-developed feeling for pace to be a good front-runner. The front-runner must be willing to ignore all diversions during the race, and even to forego a warm-up jog. The front-runner will go through the crash-point at the earliest possible time in the race—frequently as early as twelve to fifteen miles. He has to bank on wearing down his main rivals early in the race.

Among world-class marathoners, Frank Shorter, Bill Rodgers, and Canada's Jerome Drayton all favor this tactic. It's most frequently applied—with a high incidence of failure—by runners who have come to the marathon from track racing and inwardly feel the marathon is too slow . . . at least in their first race.

There are various benefits of running at the front. First of all, the leader may draw confidence and strength from the fact that he controls the pace. He has taken the initiative; the others can only follow him and prevent the formation of a gap. The longer the front-runner maintains the lead, the more nervous those following feel. If he doesn't even look back at the others, this can undermine his opponents' morale. The race leader knows at every moment what to expect ahead of him. The official vehicles pilot him over the course. To the extent that he can stay clear of exhaust fumes, this is an advantage, since he never has to run through a crowded water stop. He never loses time when he chooses to drink because he's served promptly and efficiently. He generally gets accurate split times and can hear them clearly, since all the race personnel try to do a good job for the leader. The front-runner will need splits, too, to plan the remainder of the race.

By gestures the front-runner can plant confusion and uncertainty in the minds of the following runners, for instance, by ostentatiously declining food and drinks. When he passes through the "wall," he can often hide momentary weakness or pain, from his opponents. If the front-runner has a one-minute lead during the fifteen- to twenty-one-mile phase, he can pace himself to recovery within a few miles. Thus, he can rest on his lead for a while. The crowd will tell him what's going on behind him, though half of what he's told won't be worth listening to.

One disadvantage of being a front-runner is that others are constantly challenging. The front-runner should never look around. A glance over the shoulder is a challenge to others to go past. It's an admission that the front-runner is thinking not of the road ahead but of what's behind him. Then, he becomes the hunted. If you can't keep from looking back, you should abandon front-running altogether. If the front-runner doesn't look back, he becomes the proud leader of the pack, behind whom the others must order themselves in groups. Groups are always a danger to the front-runner. Several good runners in a group can share the lead, and a group generally has a better sense of pace than the runner leading by himself. Following runners share the fears of not being able to reach the front-runner. Unless there are a lot of corners in the course, or the lead grows too large, following runners always know the exact distance between them and first place. And more often than not they'll be told the exact time elapsed between themselves the leader.

The group has an advantage in a headwind, since the wind can eat up the front-runner's energy while the runners are taking turns leading their group. Another disadvantage for the front-runner is that there may be confusion in the finish area. Even at international races someone may give the front-runner wrong directions (after the lead vehicles have already turned off the course.) Someone may tell the front-runner to take one lap too many in the stadium, as befell Waldemar Cierpinski at Montreal. Race helpers who have been waiting for hours sometimes get sleepy and do not wake up completely until a few runners have gone by.

It is clear that the front-runner has to plan his strategy with care. When the wind is gentle and the weather ideal, his chances increase. In hot weather he'll have to calculate precisely how much he will wilt in the final stages. With variable winds or questionable race organization the front-runner's chances of a start-to-finish victory begin to pale. To my way of thinking, front-running is the most beautiful way of all to win. The majestic silence that surrounds you moments after you leave the noisy starting area—and follows you for 26 miles—is a unique experience. You can only dimly hear the swelling applause of th crowds before you.

The Pack Runner

In the marathon there's no such thing as a "kicker". But there is a type of pack runner who lets himself be swept along by a group and then seizes his best chance with cold determination. The pack runner first looks over his competitors during the race, and then joins a group whose pace suits him. In an opposing wind he hides at the back of the group. When it is blowing from the left, he runs at the far right side in the wind shadow. The pack runner keeps a sharp eye out; he notices if a runner's breathing rate has suddenly risen—a sure sign of exhaustion, if a runner has a stitch, and if someone starts to sweat a lot or has stopped sweating altogether. All these things signify disadvantages for the runner's opponents and these advantages for himself. At just the right moment the pack runner will attack. It is no great risk for him to surge if his one remaining challenger is writhing with a stitch.

A pack runner usually waits until at least twenty miles into a marathon to make any kind of move; otherwise he'll have to play front-runner for too many miles.

Pack running is the most successful tactic of all. It is so common that a good two-thirds of all marathons are probably won using it. Pack running is easy on the runner's physical and psychic resources, and allows him to coast along for much of the race. The only danger is that the pack runner is always running against the true front-runner, who promptly tears the lead groups apart, leaving solo runners scattered all over the course. The typical pack runner sometimes doesn't look so good in a race like that.

The Poker Player

The British fifty-meter surge is a familiar tactic in middle-distance running. England's Rawson and Hewson won European titles in 1958 at 800 and 1,500 meters as outsiders by using this tactic. The classic short surge begins on the last turn before the finish. The runner comes out of the final curve into the last meters of the race at an accelerated speed. A kick like this will gain a lead of one or two meters, or more if the runner can deflate the others' morale.

The short sprinter will not attack again at the start of the finishing straight. He'll simply accept the loss of a meter or two, and then kick for all he's worth when he's about fifty meters from the tape. He stands a good chance of pushing himself on to a hair's-breadth victory, because the lead runner will probably not be able to counter, and may not even realize until too late that he's been challenged. The recipe was a good one for Manfred Matuschevski (nicknamed "Millimeter Matu"), who used it twice in winning the European 800-meter title, once against a stronger Franz Joseph Kemper.

In the marathon, runners of this sort may not accurately be called short sprinters; they're more like poker players. They have the ability to estimate distances with great accuracy. They're up-to-date on everything that's going on during the race, and even when they're a minute behind, they'll maintain contact with a cool, determined eye. One of the most decisive factors in marathon racing tactics is to stay in contact with runners who've jumped into the lead, but who will probably be running no faster than your own speed within a few minutes. The poker player puts his money on the flagging energies of his opponents, while banking on his own strengths.

I had good success with this tactic in 1971 at Manchester against Hans Hellbach. He is a tempo runner, and he left me soon after the start. At fifteen miles I spotted him ahead, with a sure 400- to 500-meter lead. At twenty miles I noticed that I was able to gain on him gradually, but my own cylinders were beginning to knock. At about twenty-three miles I was almost up to him, but still about twenty meters behind. He couldn't hear my footfall and couldn't tell whether his lead would grow or shrink. I knew his coach would be waiting at twenty-five miles and I wanted to avoid having him scream at Hellbach to pass me, so I stayed behind till we passed the twenty-five-mile mark. His coach had barely announced, "Twenty meters on him—you can do it!" when I pulled out all the stops. In 500 meters I'd caught Hellbach and he let me go by without a challenge; he even gave me a friendly pat on the back. If I'd passed Hellbach at twenty-three miles, it might have cost me so much strength that he'd have hung on and then been able to shake me off in the last mile. That was a case of successfully playing one's cards close to one's chest. In international racing, Belgium's Karel Lismont (European marathon champion in 1971, silver medalist at the 1972 Olympic marathon, and third at Montreal in 1976) often uses this tactic.

The risks are many. In 1973 in Germany, I dropped out of a marathon for the only time in my life for nonphysical reasons purely because I was completely deflated to learn that Lutz

Philipp's lead had grown to two miles, while I was back in fourth position playing poker.

Christa Vahlensieck won the 1976 women's international marathon at Waldniel by an unplanned poker tactic. Kim Merritt's vigorous pace seemed unbeatable. A surge at seventeen miles accomplished nothing for Christa and so, 100 meters behind, she contented herself waiting for Kim to show a weakness. When Christa passed her opponent at twenty-two miles, Kim was thoroughly beaten. This case illustrates the kind of situation for which poker-playing tactics are best suited: when the leader is an overpowering tempo runner. Generally it's not something you plan in advance, and it's always applied during the final third of the race.

Vary Your Tactics

Jumping off to an early lead, running in the pack, and chasing from behind are the three useful styles of marathon strategy. It will remain thus as long as men have legs and run races. The successful marathoner needs to master all the tactical variations as early as possible in his career. If he limits himself to copying what others are doing in a race, he's lost. If a runner has had good success as a tempo runner in the smaller world of track racing and then moves up into races of greater distances, he'll probably be forced into the role of inconspicuous pack runner or chaser. Gunther Mielke is typical of a runner who failed internationally because he couldn't give up the habit of mixing it up at the front. He was on the West German Olympic team, running the 10,000 meters in 1972 and the marathon in 1976.

You can practice the basic tactical variations while training. If you incline toward running in the pack you'll need to set yourself more difficult training tasks such as frequent solo time trials. If you prefer running alone, you'll need to get used to running in the pack with others, including the inevitable wheezing, spitting, talkative chap who you cannot allow to get on your nerves, provoking you into an early strength-sapping breakaway.

The tactician needs to free himself from dependence on the stopwatch. Only a good eye can help the pack runner or the poker player. One learns distance judgment by observing mileage markers during training runs. If you practice estimating distance (to the next turn, the next farmhouse, etc.) over and over again and then check your guesses, you'll be able to tell precisely when a racing opponent ahead of you has gained five yards.

I will conclude with a few tactical suggestions for coaches and handlers. Do not ever lie; always tell the truth. The coach who thinks he's doing his protege a favor by understating an opponent's lead is merely shortsighted. Remarks like, "He's got a helluva stitch!" may tempt one's own man into a very ill-advised move. When he then fails to gain ground on the lead runner, the effect of the misleading remark may be the opposite of what was intended. For instance, the runner may think, "He's got a bad stitch and I'm not two steps up on him. What's the use?" The runner should be thoroughly informed of the actual weaknesses of his opponents, and should be warned about opponents moving up strongly from behind.

You don't help your own man by proclaiming his weaknesses: "Five guys behind and they all look fresher than you!" This isn't the way to extend a runner's crash point. It would be more suitable to say: "You can do it now!" or "Now you can start picking it up a little!" or "You never know, that guy might start fading pretty soon!" The worst thing of all for an athlete who's going through a bad stretch is to be left all alone. He feels abandoned and doubly lonely then.

If you're operating with split times, whether as a runner or as a roadside attendant, you should be constantly working out estimates for the remainder of the race, based on actual splits and pace. Meaningful numbers that tell the story of the progress of the race make it much easier to plan ahead. Such figures are easy to hold in your mind while running, and they give you a continuous update of your strengths or weaknesses on a particular day, allowing you to plan accordingly.

The best marathon runners know all the tactical subtlties and how to put them into practice, as well as how to know an opponent's plans. (After all, in the marathon there's plenty of time to figure it out.) Abebe Bikila was cut from this mold. He paid less heed to split times than to listening to his own inner promptings. He was no slave of the clock, but its master, freed from a burden that most world-class runners cannot do without.

Chapter 22

Healing Aches and Pains

If all people were marathoners, all the medical internists would be back in school learning another specialty—orthopedics. The orthopedist—the bone, tendon, and joint doctor—is the only kind of physician whose office the marathon runner is likely to step inside. Injuries are far less common in runners than those of speed-and-strength athletes. Sudden accidents, tears, and breaks are almost unknown among runners. When they happen the damage is due to accumulated endurance stresses, rather than running itself. Degenerative damage doesn't occur in running. At most, a preexisting condition will come to the fore through training.

The injuries of marathon runners can be placed in three categories:

- inflammation of the Achilles tendon
- knee pain
- rheumatic complaints like arthritis and sciatica

First let's discuss minor aches and pains, such as muscle soreness. A lot of marathon runners are surprised that they become sore after hard runs, even after daily training. Muscle soreness is unavoidable; it results from overacidification of the muscles caused by depletion of electrolytes and by hard muscle effort. At speeds faster than a 2:40 marathon pace, in particular, the foot strikes the pavement so hard that the running motion can no longer be cushioned. The decreased local muscle endurance leads to soreness. In extremely severe cases soreness can last for a week following a hard marathon race.

Muscle soreness is treated using the same movements that

caused it. I have always admired the runner who gets up early the day after a marathon for an easy hour's run. His iron self-discipline helps the body get rid of accumulated waste products. A long run a half-day after a marathon race is good also because muscle soreness has not yet fully set in then. But I've never been able to generate the energy to do this. On principle, I never run the day after a marathon; for once I just turn the whole business off. However, a morning run the day after a marathon is ideal for quick muscle recovery.

In some cases, muscle soreness becomes so severe two days after a marathon that the runner has difficulty even walking upstairs. When he tries to run every step may hurt. There are methods to help you even if you're in this dire extremity. Take a hot epsom-salts bath—as hot as you can stand it. Massage your legs with a deep–heating balm before beginning, and then run in place on a soft carpet until you feel some improvement. You might take magnesium pills, since they are the most effective means of breaking down lactic acid in the muscles. In the period just after a race or after a hard training phase resulting in muscle soreness, there is danger of muscle tears and small strains. Cramping can also lead to minor ruptures. This is a time when the runner should go slow and do all his running on flat courses, taking jogging pauses when desired. Muscle tears are nearly unknown in long-distance runners, though they are quite common among sprinters.

The only fractures that occur in road running are fatigue breaks, which most commonly involve the toes or the middle foot. This is, of course, more frightening to the victim, but it should not sour him altogether on running. In such cases the runner has usually increased his mileage too quickly, ignoring foot pain. Fatigue fractures are especially common among women, whose feet are less flexible than men's. Nearly all men have played at least a little touch football in school, but women over thirty may have done little sports activity in their lives, making them the most vulnerable beginners of all. Joan Ullyot, for example, had several stress fractures before she finally acquired a degree of immunity and went on to become a world-class runner.

Objections to Injections

Now we come to the most common, annoying, and long-lasting runner's injury: Achilles tendinitis. The runner feels severe pain between calf and heel bone, with redness that comes for awhile, fades, and then returns more pronounced than before. The pain while running is often unbearable, and the desire to run is correspondingly low. Many a physician who sees tendinitis quickly reaches for the syringe—usually one filled with cortisone. If he's not up-to-date on athletic injuries he'll inject directly into the tendon. This is now considered the wrong practice, however, because the danger of actual tears in the Achilles tendon rises with each new injection. It could even be said that this form of treatment is the major cause of Achilles tears. Though I'm not a physician, I can only warn my fellow runners to change to another doctor as soon as possible if he tries to inject anything into the Achilles.

The average doctor will advise immediate cessation of exercise, just as he would for any other injury. This may or may not be good advice, as improved circulation while running can accelerate the cure. If the runner takes a break from training he'll probably experience pain when he tries to start running again. Thus, by taking the path of least resistance, the runner may never get through the pain barrier, but may instead consider himself chronically injured.

I recommend endurance running, as slow as possible and by no means at one's regular training pace or mileage. Also use wet wraps at night, rubbing the leg with heating liniment, wrapping it in wet towels, and then covering the wet wrap with a loose plastic cloth to keep the body's natural heat concentrated in the wet towels and to accelerate recovery through improved circulation. Many doctors and masseurs use cold sprays for the first twenty-four hours after the symptoms appear. Heat should be applied only when the pain is receding. There are a number of hot salves you can try before reaching for the hard stuff. Plaster casts are totally unneeded for treating Achilles tendinitis. A cast will only cause the foot and calf muscles to atrophy and will leave the patient standing on a scrawny chicken leg that he may reinjure when the cast is removed.

Preventing Achilles tendon injuries is even more important. If you can listen to what your body is telling you, you'll make appropriate changes when little irritations first appear, thus preventing minor inflammations from developing into major problems. The chief causes of tendinitis are: poor shoes, high body weight, and overtraining. Variations in running terrain can also lead to tendinitis (for example, from roads to the soft sand of a beach during summer vacation, or from the cinder track to forest paths). If you are not used to wearing spikes and put on a pair to race on the track, the reward will often be severe Achilles pain. Be careful when even minor swelling appears in the Achilles region. Start treatment with cold sprays and wet wraps, and cut back mileage for a few days. If the tendon hurts, always keep training on hard, flat surfaces; do not, as is often advised, run on soft grass or forest paths.

There is a danger here. Runners will try to protect their injured Achilles tendon while running on hard (and perhaps unfamiliar) surfaces by favoring the healthy leg. This can cause knee injuries, which are aggravated by running on hard surfaces. The runner with knee problems needs a soft surface.

Arrange for frequent changes in running surface during training runs; look for rolling terrain so your pace will vary naturally. Change shoes frequently, wearing different styles and brands to vary the stresses on your feet. Whenever I've trained three times a day, I've changed shoes for each workout. I've arrived at training camps with five different pairs of shoes and have always sadly shaken my head seeing fellow runners using the same one or two pairs. They had less baggage, but they also carried more salves, tinctures, and pills to treat their little aches and pains.

As long as the pain comes only while you're running, you can help matters with a little warm-up routine. Before you go out for your training run, run fifteen minutes with the sole purpose of reaching the point where your Achilles pain begins to fade. Then wait for as long as an hour. When you go out for your regular run, you'll sometimes find there's no pain at all.

I recommend shoes with well-made heels that are not too low. High heel cups that rub the Achilles should be cut off the day you buy the shoes, or else these shoes should not be worn. Avoid all hard intervals and sudden accelerations in training; make your speed changes flowing and gradual.

The Knee—Nature's Mistake?

Some physicians consider the knee a gigantic error in mechanical design, unsuitable for the upright locomotion of two-legged animals. True or not, this complicated leg hinge is both a point of friction in human forward movement and the subject of innumerable medical diagnoses. This area is so confusing that I prefer to just pass on the views of Dr. van Aaken, who has treated more than 3,000 patients with knee pain. Van Aaken considers the most common injuries to be an inflammation of the fatty material between kneecap and shin bone. Though it isn't well known in medical circles, this syndrome occurs with great frequency in runners, and is often wrongly diagnosed as arthrosis, meniscus damage, or any number of other ailments.

I used to have regular knee trouble after every break in training or in the easy recovery phase, but it usually disappeared within a week or two. There's usually minor swelling that may look like internal hemmorhaging. The knee makes a crackling sound and movement is hampered. My simple, but effective, therapy was to keep running—perhaps with a faster, longer stride and on softer surfaces. Dr. van Aaken recommends hot baths with table salt and a sulfate solution added.

The best-known knee injury is meniscus damage, so common among soccer players that it is considered an occupational hazard of the sport; it is less common among distance runners. Meniscus damage is due less to the structure of the human knee than to the sideways movements common in soccer. Meniscus damage in runners occurs almost exclusively from uncontrolled sideways movements in cross-country running, and from falls during training runs. There are naturally more complex knee injuries as well. But their diagnosis and treatment is best left to the experienced sports physician.

Sciatica and Cold Showers

From what has been said so far, the reader should realize that I am extremely skeptical when it comes to prescribing medications. No effect can be achieved with medications without side effects. Pain can be temporarily dulled with pills, but the body must fight its own illnesses. This is especially true of the increasingly frequent rheumatic diseases. Inflammation of the joints, sciatica, and lumbago are on the increase. While many physicians attribute this to excessive irritation from exercise, Dr. van Aaken disagrees. Dr. Otto Brucker points out that we are living in an age when people are exercising less than ever; yet they are afflicted with unprecedented levels of rheumatic disease. Many runners are frightened into leaving the sport by a diagnosis of "arthrosis." Brucker says that the rheumatic diseases do not result from too much movement, but from decades of improper diet. Brucker makes a connection between rheumatic syndromes and the catastrophic state of civilized man's teeth. He recommends a full-value diet devoid of refined sugars, but rich in vegetable protein. He feels that this alone will prevent rheumatic problems.

The most common injury of this type in the road runner is a pinched sciatic nerve, which can cause pain that may radiate over the entire buttocks, to the kidneys or deep into the upper thighs. The pain is a continuous irritation, and in severe cases is present while sitting as well as standing. It is a great obstacle to a fluid running style. Nevertheless, it is possible to keep on running in spite of sciatica.

I have had long experience with sciatica, especially during months of high mileage. For some time I felt that an injection two weeks before an important race once a year was the only way to continue training and racing at my normal level. But after awhile I was thoroughly fed up with dependence on shots, and began experimenting with natural cures. A sauna gave me some relief, but when I tried bathing in cold water I found the cure. I needed no more injections and no more pills—only a piece of sawed-off garden hose with which I poured cold water over myself. I followed the rules of the Kneipp baths, which Dr. Brucker highly recommends. I've found that the sudden cold and subsequent counter-reaction caused by this method increased internal circulation, warming the critical areas.

Sciatica symptoms certainly result from running, because they immediately diminish when the runner reduces mileage for a few weeks. But are they caused by hard pounding on the pavement, by the skin-cooling effects of sweat evaporation, or by atrophy of the back muscles? No one knows for certain—or, at least, everyone has a different answer. But it is not harmful to try the sauna, the cold baths, and massage, along with special exercise for the back muscles. (You could add a few foot exercises for the prevention of Achilles tendinitis.)

If you can master these cures and keep a low power-to-weight ratio, the diseases described can be avoided (or at least will not keep you from running). Note that getting injured is not a passive process; the runner himself is ultimately the source of his own injuries.

Chapter 23

High Altitude Training

Ever since the 1968 Olympic Games in Mexico City, magazines, newspapers, and athletic journals have been discussing high-altitude training, altitude anxiety, and the incommensurable advantages of high-altitude dwellers over flatlanders. Expensive expeditions were mounted to take national teams to the pre-Olympic meets in Mexico in 1966 and 1967. The German teams returned with inconclusive evidence. The German middle- and long-distance specialists, with the exception of Bodo Tummler (who won a bronze in the 1,500 meters in 1968), generally failed to adapt to altitude. Sports medicine had few prescriptions for running at high altitude. Even Arnd Kruger, who'd been racing at 1,500 meters and training in Mexico for a full year prior to the Games, was eliminated in the heats. English schoolteacher Tim Johnston, who had also been teaching in Mexico for a year, finished eighth in the Games' marathon.

African runners won all the races of 1,500 meters and longer. When the African successes were not repeated at Munich in 1972 and the Africans boycotted the Montreal Games for political reasons—making evaluation of their current progress difficult—altitude training was gradually forgotten. In England there was also the memory of disastrous altitude training at St. Moritz in 1972, which resulted in disappointing performances, especially by Dave Bedford.

But one thing was forgotten. The African runners' advantage had been balanced at Munich by the numerous world-class athletes who had gone to high altitude for long-distance training and then had returned to perform magnificently in the

Games. Frank Shorter, for instance, lived for a long time at high altitude before winning the 1972 Olympic marathon, and again before finishing second at Montreal. For at least several months before a big race he lives and trains at his parents' home in Colorado, training at altitudes higher than 6,500 feet. Shorter is always trying to talk other American world-class runners into training at high altitude. Finnish stars Juha Vaatainen (1971 double European champion) and Lasse Viren (twice Olympic gold medalist in 1972 and 1976) have spent a good deal of time far from Finland in the high-altitude areas of Kenya and Colombia.

Dozens of scientific papers have been published on altitude training. French researchers from Font Romeu in the Pyrenees (more than 6,100 feet) are of the opinion that athletes should train for a full year at 10,000 feet. If the athletes later return to sea level, say the scientists, they will be ready to improve on the world records. Professor Harald Mellerowicz of Berlin found in tests with identical twins that the siblings who trained at high altitude had an advantage. He said it was still uncertain whether blood hemoglobin levels could be influenced by training at high altitude. For years, increased hemoglobin counts were considered the main advantage of training in the mountains; but now this has been attacked scientifically.

The classical assumption is that training for two or three weeks at high altitude results in the following significant improvements:

- a percentage rise in hemoglobin, the oxygen-transport mechanism of the blood
- an improvement in lung capacity and oxygen transport to the cells
- an increase in myoglobin in the muscle
- a subjective sensation of well-being at borderline stress four to ten days after returning to sea level, with the ability to maintain a relatively fast pace with a good margin to spare and to mount a long sprint during the final phases of the race

The last point shows that science does not present us with well-defined procedures. The feeling that one can maintain a certain pace without having to breathe hard is probably due more to psychological factors than to actual physical improvement.

I am convinced of the value of altitude training, not just for world-class athletes, but also for attaining general fitness. This is based on my own training experiences in St. Moritz, Font Romeu, Mexico, Colombia, and even a 3,000-meter race in La Paz, Bolivia, at 13,000 feet. Many athletes made errors while preparing for the high-altitude Olympics in Mexico. For one thing, they had scarcely any racing experiences at high altitude. This put them at a definite disadvantage vis-à-vis the African runners, and definitely limited their tactical options and pace judgment. In the second place, Mexico, at 7,500 feet, would not have seemed so awesome after a few weeks of training at even higher altitudes. This is exactly what the Kenyans and Ethiopians did, even though they already lived at altitudes equal to that of Mexico City. The Brazilian world-champion soccer team prepared for the 1970 World Cup matches in Mexico by training at Bogota, Colombia, about 1,200 feet higher than Mexico City. A third error many athletes make who train at altitude is that they do not plan their training mileage in an appropriate fashion. Finally, many athletes underestimate other climatic factors, such as adaptation to high relative humidity when returning to lower altitudes. Training at high altitude during spring or early summer at European resorts can also be interrupted by sudden cold spells.

I recommend the following preparation at high altitude for the marathon, for both world-class athletes and average runners. If you train at high altitude in Europe, plan to stay at least three weeks. Less is useless, because it takes at least a week to get acclimatized to the point where the circulatory system reacts normally. Frequently there's a minor crisis after twelve to fourteen days, though this passes quickly. Training longer than this is not good either, as living in high-altitude resorts, such as Font Romeu or even St. Moritz, becomes boring in summer.

Altitude training—effective only above 6,000 feet—can be continued in the French and Swiss Alps, the Carpathian Mountains, in villages of the Spanish Sierra Nevada, and in the Caucasus, where the Soviet high-altitude center is located at Erevan. Outside Europe, high-altitude training can be done on the island of Tenerife, in Mexico, Colombia, and in the United States. South American countries are especially recommended for high-altitude training during the Northern Hemisphere winter.

The question of how to do altitude training is just as important as where to do it. Most runners believe they need to bring their aerobic capacity to maximum levels in a short period of time at high altitude. Then they overextend themselves and get into anaerobic stress, because the oxygen in the air is 5 to 10 percent less concentrated than at sea level. Inevitably, they end up overtrained. Instead of building condition, they reach dangerously deep into their reserves. Then when they return to flat country and perform poorly, they blame altitude training for their lack of success. Runners who do a lot of hard intervals and fast-paced running are especially vulnerable. Since British runners trained in this style at St. Moritz in 1972, they were particularly "soured" when running for the medals at Munich.

The marathon runner should think: "At a 5 to 10 percent slower pace I'll be doing the same work I'd be doing at normal altitudes. At the same time, I'll be giving my leg muscles, joints, and tendons a rest by running slower. I can therefore run more miles without risk of injury." This is the secret of the successes of Gaston Roelants, who at thirty-eight finished third at the 1974 European Championships in Rome.

A danger at high altitude is that, lacking flat loop courses, the runner may be forced to run frequently on variable courses involving significant changes in altitude. A little mountain lake that the runner can circle while training is an ideal site. Besides this venue, the runner should seek out even higher altitudes of 8,500 to 9,000 feet, particularly during the first days. There, the runner should do slow endurance runs with no time goals. Enormous increases in pulse rate—up to 200 beats per minute—are the rule during the initial days. You can also expect a flickering, then racing, pulse during the recovery phase before training stresses are completely assimilated. Resting pulse will rise in the first days, but will eventually return to levels lower than normal for running on the flat.

It is a mistake to assume that a runner can begin high-altitude training in poor condition and then return fit to low altitude running. High-altitude work demands that the runner arrive in fit condition with the purpose of further developing his form. I also have doubts about the effectiveness of altitude training for people over fifty years old; they may be in superb condition but their adaptive processes are slower. An untrained person should not begin marathon training at high altitude.

It is important, too, to know when and how to return. A race four days after training at altitude may be fine for the 1,500-meter or 5,000-meter specialist, but not for the marathoner. Higher oxygen uptake does not make a decisive difference for the marathoner. He can thus wait a while before racing, because the significant altitude effects for the marathoner will stay with him for weeks. It is more important for the marathon runner to readapt to low-altitude climatic conditions after he is used to pure, thin, low-humidity mountain air—which is more conducive to good performance. My advice is to train at high altitude in August to run a best time in a September or October marathon.

Chapter 24

Training for the 100-Kilometer Run

It is easier to run 100 kilometers (62 miles) than it is to run the marathon. Furthermore, it's not just subjectively easier, it's actually easier on the muscles and internal organs.

Fifteen or twenty years ago it was inconceivable that the 100-kilometer run would ever become a mass sport. The first 100-kilometer race on the European continent was held at Biel, Switzerland, in 1959 with twenty-two starters and a winning time of 13 hours, 45 minutes. Like many other athletic events in Switzerland, the 100-kilometer race had its origin in the military. Franz Reist, an army major, is still president of the organizing committee. In the meantime, the race fields at Biel have grown to nearly 4,000. The race starts at 10 p.m. and the runners take off into the night, which in itself is a psychological advantage. With the rising sun, just about when the runners have reached their crash point, things begin to look up. The leaders arrive in marathoning attire; and the last timed runners—mostly stouthearted hikers in full dress carrying loaded ruck-sacks—cross the line in twenty-four hours.

A 100-kilometer race can be run at 50 percent of maximal speed. This figure comes from statistical analyses of race fields, as well as from the experiments Professor Nowacki performed in Giessen, Germany, which showed that a person can maintain 50 percent of maximal exercise levels for 8 hours. Nowacki's test results are borne out by actual race data.

Pace in the 100-kilometer race is so slow compared with the marathon that muscle and liver glycogen is not used to any significant extent. The 100-kilometer runner uses his fat reserves from the beginning of the race to the finish. In the marathon, fats are not burned until about twenty-two miles, since fat metabolism is uneconomical at the fast racing speeds of the shorter, 26-mile race. For the 100 kilometers, however, fat is exactly what is needed. Unlike glycogen metabolism, fat metabolism does not have to be adapted to borderline stress levels. For this reason, it is possible to run 100 kilometers on relatively little training. In addition, organic stresses and muscle strain are lower in the 100 kilometers than in the marathon. The runner who encounters a true physical crisis in the 100 kilometers will prefer to drop out, considering the gigantic distance involved and the risk of serious physical damage.

Aside from the great physical output required to complete 100 kilometers, the main prerequisite is the psychological toughness to survive the distance. Though 100 kilometers would be beyond the reach of the average runner in training, the mass of runners in the race encourage a favorable mood and provide running partners for just about everyone. A buddy will help you when things are not going well, or you may be able to cheer up someone else, forgetting your own troubles in the process. More friendships are formed in the 100-kilometer run than on a bus ride home from work. Whole life stories have been exchanged during the race.

Calorie Requirements

Despite its relatively slow pace, the calorie requirements for the 100-kilometer race are huge—much higher than for the marathon. The average caloric demand for 100 kilometers is 6,000. For the finish times between 6½ and 8 hours the calorie requirements are about the same, so no energy is saved at all by running slower within this time frame. This may explain why top runners can run the first half much faster than the second half without risking a later physical collapse.

A 200-pounder, at a complete disadvantage in the marathon, will be equally excluded from the front of the field in the 100 kilometers. But he will be able to finish the distance with a little training. (His calorie consumption will be 8,000 to 9,000.) Only with extremely low body weight does the caloric requirements for the 100 kilometers fall below 5,000. This is why it is absolutely essential to take in nutrients during the race.

First the 100—Then the Marathon

One need not follow the usual pattern and graduate from shorter to longer to run the 100 kilometers. While it requires at least a year to prepare for the marathon, it takes only six months to prepare for the 100-kilometer run.

It's much easier to run and walk 100 kilometers in fourteen hours (averaging about 4-1/3 miles per hour, or a 14-minute mile) than it is to run the marathon in less than four hours. The fellow who's running the marathon in six hours, on the wings of a dream of someday really running the 26 miles, would actually be better off just letting the marathon ride for awhile and turning his attention to the 100 kilometers. The 100 kilometers is billed as a "hike or run"; in France the term is *à style libre*. A runner will always be faster than a walker at 100 kilometers, so the ideal is to run the 100 kilometers, even if one is a beginner.

This is why I advise the older first-timer who is attracted to long road events to first choose the 100 kilometers, and then wait until he is in good enough condition to break five hours before attempting the marathon or shorter road races at six to fifteen miles. These shorter races won't take him as close to his maximal performance limits as the marathon, but they will help prepare his muscles and internal organs for the 26 miles.

The training of a 100-kilometer runner is not all that different from that of a marathoner. Just do more miles, and do them slower. Only world-class runners with eight-hour potential need to run thirty miles or longer regularly in training, and even then only once every week or two. Runners who want to break 7 hours should do 180 miles a week. England's Ron Bentley, who holds the world record for the 24-hour run, did weeks of up to 250 miles, or an average of thirty-five-plus miles per day, during his prerace training. For the average 100-kilometer runner, such training mileage is, of course, unthinkable and unnecessary. Two long runs in training at distances longer than the marathon are enough to provide motivation for the race, when the runner will be pulled along by the field.

There are 100-kilometer runners who train less than marathoners—only two or three times a week—and who stay in condition by racing frequently at distances of 100 kilometers or less. This is explained by the less-demanding energy requirements of the 100-kilometer event as compared with the marathon. One of the greatest living 100-kilometer specialists, Helmut Urbach of Cologne, trains in this way. Urbach has won the Biel race five times and holds the unofficial world record on the roads at 6:40:03. Heinz Hasler of Switzerland has run faster, but this was under questionable conditions. Urbach races every chance he can get, but trains little during the week, possible because of heavy physical labor on his job as a lathe hand. Because of his light training, Urbach's organic adaptation is not as good as it could be, and his marathon potential is similarly untapped. This is quite evident on short hills, where Urbach rapidly gets into trouble. But he compensates by going fast downhill, something his extraordinarily insensitive feet allow him to do. He has the typical uncomplicated attitude of the endurance-type runner, arriving at races at the last minute and eating the first thing he's handed. Considering his amazing recovery ability, he must be something of an "enzyme giant." After a 100-kilometer run, which he claims is easier for him than the marathon, he claims to experience no muscle soreness. Like many other 100-kilometer runners, he has such a high level of hormone activity after a race that he feels no fatigue and sleeps no longer than usual. Urbach has run a marathon in close to his best time just a week after a difficult 100-kilometer race. But Urbach's training methods are only a qualified success, as he has numerous "flops" during the second half of the season, when he frequently does not go the distance.

A runner cast in a different mold is Serge Cottereau, a French physical education teacher born in 1938, who once ran on French international teams at the middle distances before switching to the 100 kilometers. Cottereau won the Millau 100 kilometers five years in a row, and has written a book, *Le Grand Fond à Style Libre*. Published in 1975, it is the first book in French on ultradistance running.

Cottereau drew up the following simple nine-month training plan culminating in a fifteen-hour, 100-kilometer run:

first month   once a week, 1 hour
second month twice a week, 1 hour

third month	once a week, 1 hour
	once a week, 1½ hours
fourth month	once a week, 1 hour
	once a week, 2 hours
fifth month	once a week, 1 hour
	once a week, 2:15
sixth month	once a week, 1 hour
	once a week, 2:45
seventh month	twice a week, 1 hour
	once a week, 3:00
eighth month	twice a week, 1 hour
	once a week, 3:15
ninth month	twice a week, 1 hour
	once a week, 3:30

This is a beginner's training program for the jogger who's going straight into the 100-kilometers, bypassing track racing and the marathon. Naturally, one can try to run three or four times a week instead of just twice. If the runner does this, it is only necessary to run longer than an hour once a week to reach the fifteen-hour goal. Cottereau, who came from the middle distances, also gives detailed training plans for the runner coming to long distance from the track. He writes: "Your biggest handicap is style. You have an impressive but uneconomical style, and the first consideration in ultradistance running is economy. It's useless to lift your knees and feet high off the ground. Try to run with the least-possible visual effect— your feet should glide over the ground. If you don't succeed in this, don't get upset, it'll come with time. . . . "

World-class runners training for 100 kilometers should often train at race pace, in contrast with marathoners, who must often train slower than race pace. This will give the runner an especially good feeling for time and rhythm, which he'll need during the critical interval between thirty-five and fifty miles (sixty to eighty kilometers), when he can quickly lose minutes.

Cottereau provides a useful training plan for world-class runners, presumably the one he followed. The basis of his plan is six runs a week, with fifteen hours of running during the intensive phase. He recommends four or five training runs of four to five hours duration during the year—apparently assuming there will be only one 100-kilometer race per year. The last training of this type is done three weeks before the race.

The schedule for the final two weeks before a 100-kilometer race for a world-class runner is as follows:

FIRST WEEK

Sunday	3½ hours
Monday	1 hour
Tuesday	2½ hours
Wednesday	1 hour
Thursday	2 hours
Friday	1½ hours
Saturday	1 hour

SECOND WEEK

Sunday	1½ hours
Monday	1 hour
Tuesday	1½ hours
Wednesday	45 minutes
Thursday	45 minutes
Friday	45 minutes
Saturday	30-35 minutes

Clothing for the Long Distance

The equipment for running 100 kilometers is quite different from that for a marathon. First of all, the 100-kilometer runner should not run in his fastest shoes, but rather in the oldest pair he owns. If they have been patched several times and look like they're going to fall apart any minute, they're just right. They won't be too tight, they won't cause blisters, and the sweat will run out the holes. The only thing new on the shoes should be the laces.

The runner's clothing should be made of cotton. The elastic band in the shorts should not be too tight, and there should be a lining in them. The upper dress is a problem. There can sometimes be radical changes in the weather during a race, with temperatures varying twenty to thirty degrees. A net shirt is recommended only for morning starts. The combination of net shirt and T-shirt is good, since the T-shirt can be removed later (once the problem of attaching the race number has been solved). Surprisingly, newspaper is a superb reserve item of clothing. When it's cold or rainy, newpaper will protect you; just put it in your shorts, front or back. The advantage is that you can throw away rain- or sweat-soaked newspaper in any corner litter basket, and it's a great insulator. Racing cyclists stuff newspapers in their jerseys to keep from catching cold while descending Alpine passes after long climbs. In extreme weather this trick can also be used in the marathon. There is still more to be learned from the racing cyclist. Instead of a normal track singlet, I recommend that runners wear the road cyclist's long-sleeved cotton jersey with two hind pockets. A cycling cap is useful in the chill of night, as well as in the heat of the day. A handkerchief and toilet paper (last but not least!) are important items of equipment. If a handler is available, he should have a complete fresh set of clothing ready—at least fresh wool socks, and if possible a rainproof anorak for the cold. The handler takes care of food, a sponge, or a wet handkerchief, and should be familiar with a few massage techniques. Finally, it's advisable for the runner racing at distances beyond twenty-five miles to take some nourishment every six miles.

The veteran runner has a great opportunity in the 100-kilometer run. He may never fully realize his performance potential until reaching forty. An especially remarkable case is that of Rosa Vogeli of Biel, who one day got tired of sitting and watching while her sons raced. At seventy years of age she entered the 100 kilometers for the first time and has been a regular at the Biel race ever since.

Rosa Vogeli's performances, plus the world-class 7:50:38 run by Christa Vahlensieck in 1976, testify to the potential of women in the 100 kilometers. Slower basic speed is not a factor at 100 kilometers, while favorable power-to-weight ratio and the specific female metabolic advantages become especially significant. Christa Vahlensieck, who ran through the appropriate splits until sixty kilometers finished fourth in a field of 700 men. It won't be long before more women are running under eight hours in the 100 kilometers. The fastest possible time for a woman is probably around seven hours. Vahlen-sieck's race with no special preparation (only two prior runs beyond the marathon distance) hints at what male world-class marathoners could do if they committed themselves to training for the 100 kilometers. If training was better, the world track record, a 6:32 by England's Kevin Woodward, would surely soon be improved.

The 100-kilometer distance can be measured on the roads with the same precision that prevails for the marathon. In any case, a great human experience like this belongs not in the musty narrowness of a stadium, but rather in the open country-side.

Chapter 25

Your Body Is Your Capital

"Daily long runs are my daily medical exam." So says Peter Middel, the twenty-seven-year-old editor of Germany's leading distance running magazine, *Spiridon*. Middel discovered a hidden inflammation of the heart muscle at its first appearance while running, and got treatment for it before more severe symptoms developed. Similarly, former German 5,000-meter titlist Werner Girke suffered a rare infectious disease of the lung. After finishing poorly in two races he was examined at the Freiburg University Clinic, and the ailment was discovered. If he hadn't been running, the disease might not have been discovered until too late. A former work colleague of mine died of undiagnosed diabetes. Seemingly vigorous, but overweight and a drinker, he blamed all his symptoms on overwork and alcohol. At forty, he reached the end of his road. It was too late for insulin.

Civilization, hand-in-hand with its readily available poisons, is robbing man of innumerable physical perceptions: of the sensation and internal feelings through limbs and organs. Nowadays we are aware of our insides only when they begin to hurt. But the body is man's greatest resource; it is intended to be more than an empty shell through which he pumps drugs and alcohol for the "expansion of consciousness." Exhilaration need not be forced into the bloodstream by injection. It can grow from the inside outward—and does so when our cells are permeated by oxygen carried by the bloodstream.

The running high comes when speed and rhythm focus the runner's perceptions of beautiful surroundings, and is a legitimate form of consciousness expansion. This feeling is

189

unknown to the flipped-out drug user staring at his barren walls. The body's health does not suffer to pay for the running high; on the contrary, the trained body pays off with rich dividends. But at the same time, the euphoric feelings of distance running are similar to sensations artificially induced by alcohol and hashish. This begins with increased carbon dioxide in the brain—in one case produced by toxic substances, and in the marathon by exercise at the threshold between aerobic and anaerobic pace. The high gives a runner wings, as his purely physical effort steadily increases, and then tapers off at last to a pleasant fatigue.

It's easy to see how the marathoner does without drugs. He knows another kind of high: the rhythm of his own footfall. In races, the marathoner is like the actor who performs beyond himself under the magnetic stimulus of thousands of eyes, sucking up applause like nectar. During the great city marathons, like Boston and New York, even the last plodder knows that the crowds are cheering him on.

The typical marathoner is neither an ascetic nor a masochist; he just enjoys what he's doing. One of his great pleasures in daily running is to breathe deeply and full, running his lungs through their scales like a singer. Smoking and running would be as unsatisfying as the Mexican two-step—one step forward and one step back. Hard liquor isn't favored by the marathoner, either; increasingly, he inclines offers of it. The fact that many marathoners can empty one pitcher of beer after the other is due to heavy water losses, as well as the obvious advantages of this drink. A cocktail party of marathoners, on the other hand, is something that just doesn't happen (though I should qualify this statement to recommend drinking a glass of schnapps before a race in 5-below weather for improved circulation).

The marathoner has his body well under control. This gives him a decided advantage in life. He knows how much he can do physically, and in many ways he's able to transfer his athletic abilities into the occupational or private sphere. He becomes skeptical about blind acceptance of the automation of our lives and he is wide awake to assaults on the environment. The marathoner is aware that his car can take him quickly into beautiful running country, but he also knows that the auto is the reason he doesn't like to run around his own block. Though he knows that intense perspiration drives environmental poisons out of his system faster than his inactive neighbor can eliminate them, he is aware that if he runs next to the freeway he assimilates lead, which cannot be metabolized by the body.

Balance and rhythm make the true marathoner. He is known by his avoidance of unnecessary stress situations in both training and competition. If he does get into high-stress situations, he's proceeding on a false assumption; snatch-and grab is not the name of the marathoning game. The runner must glide into his effort and become one with the road. This attitude is non-European in its essence, and corresponds more closely to the Asian mentality. This attitude is healthier and more sparing of the nerves. (This is a hint, perhaps, at the reason why Asians of the temperate zone—the Japanese and Koreans—are such good marathoners.)

The marathon runner counts his capital not in houses and cars, but in the reserves of his own body. Yet he does well by himself, too. Rising health-care costs tell even the man who's nailed fast to the dollar that he is wisest to let overtime and penny-pinching go, in favor of investing a few hours in his body.

But even running has its workaholics. Compulsive overachieving is as unhealthy in sports as it is in business, and should be equally avoided. This has long been recognized in athletic training theory, and most often strikes the conscientious worker who wants to excel at everything, and thus gives every new task a 100 percent effort. But there are limits. Overtraining results in rapid performance drops, in spite of steadfast training. Along with poor times come insomnia, faster resting pulse rates, and sudden weight losses. The way out of this kind of stress syndrome is, first, to limit your racing; second, to do only slow endurance running; and third, to watch your weight and resting pulse continuously (taken every morning before getting out of bed). If necessary, take a complete layoff. Arthur Lydiard, the great running coach from New Zealand, says that a day's training lost can be made up only by two days of workouts in a row. But for the recreational runner I'm inclined to be less fanatical. The Bible says that even God rested on the seventh day. Less is sometimes more, and blind zeal only hurts.

If you run the marathon as a wholesome hobby, you can be

almost certain that the fitness you gain will extend the years of your life. The title of Dr. van Aaken's book, *Programmed for 100 Years of Living*, is not utopian. Our society has attained a high average life expectancy through lowered infant mortality and the discovery of cures for infectious disease. But there has been no increase in life expectancy for fifty to sixty-year-olds because negative factors in the environment and detrimental habits of "civilized" man have had ravaging effects on this age-group. Only if something is done to promote physical fitness in these years can we expect a positive change. And the marathon-running pioneers of age seventy and over are now setting the example. It is up to the rest of us to follow their lead.

PHOTO CREDITS

Chapter 1   Two runners nearing the end of the 1977 Boston Marathon. (Photo by Jeff Johnson)

Chapter 2   Marathoner stepping out. (Photo by Don Melandry)

Chapter 3   Two runners pacing themselves through a marathon. (Photo by Dave Drennan)

Chapter 4   Runner completes the San Francisco marathon. (Photo by Lorraine Rorke)

Chapter 5   The great Ethiopian marathoner, Abebe Bikila. (Photo by Horst Müller)

Chapter 6   A marathoner over forty goes through the paces. (Photo by H. Lawrence Greller)

Chapter 7   A woman strides through a marathon. (Photo by John Marconi)

Chapter 8   A young runner. (Photo by John Marconi)

Chapter 9   A man preparing for his first marathon with the help of a friend. (Photo by David K. Madison)

Chapter 10   Brian Maxwell strides out. (Photo by Dave Stock)

Chapter 11   Some four-hour marathoners. (Photo by Dick Berggren)

Chapter 12   Amby Burfoot at the 1978 Boston Marathon. (Photo by M.L. Thomas)

Chapter 13   Kevin Ryan and Frank Shorter at the 1978 Boston Marathon. (Photo by M.L. Thomas)

Chapter 14   Two marathoners, Gary Tuttle and Ron Wayne, at the Ohme-Hochi Marathon.

Chapter 15   Bill Rodgers, winner of the 1978 Boston Marathon. (Photo by M.L.Thomas)

Chapter 16   Bill Rodgers downs some mineral water after winning a race. (Photo by Pete Souza)

Chapter 17   A runner eating after a race. (Photo by Cathy Breitenbucher)

Chapter 18   Athol Barton, winner of the 1977 San Francisco Marathon, drinking beer. (Photo by Randolph Falk)

Chapter 19   Marathoner drinking during a race. (Photo by Jim Engle)

Chapter 20   Runner cooling down after a marathon. (Photo by Jeff Johnson)

Chapter 21   Shorter, Ryan, and Rodgers vie for position in the 1978 Boston Marathon. (Photo by M.L. Thomas)

Chapter 22   A runner's foot being taped during the 1978 Boston Marathon. (Photo by M.L. Thomas)

Other Books on Running from Anderson World

Beginner's Running Guide by Hal Higdon. Everything a beginner needs to know to get started running on the right foot can be found in this book. The author draws on 30 years running experience to give you the most up to date and comprehensive knowledge in a breezy, personal style. Hardback $12.95.

Dr. George Sheehan's Medical Advice for Runners by Dr. George Sheehan. Here's Dr. Sheehan's first book designed to help you stay injury free. Dr. Sheehan feels that many running ailments are self-inflicted and therefore are preventable if we find and eliminate the cause. Hardback $11.95.

The Complete Woman Runner by the editors of *Runner's World*. Covering everything from getting started to entering competition once the body is properly conditioned, the book also contains a section on the mind and body of the woman runner: her potential and aptitudes. Hardback $12.00.

Jog, Run, Race by Joe Henderson. Leads the reader through several new beginnings—from walking to jogging, jogging to running, running to racing. Each beginning has a specific day by day progress guide. Hardback $6.95, Paperback $5.95.

The Complete Diet Guide: For Runners and Other Athletes from the editors of *Runner's World*. How the athlete can use his diet to better advantage is the basis of this book. Areas addressed: weight control, drinks, fasting, natural vs. processed food, vegetarian diets and more. Paperback $5.95.

The Complete Marathoner edited by Joe Henderson. Written by top marathoners, this book offers advice for both the veteran and the first-time marathoner. There is emphasis on training, racing and nutrition. Hardback $11.95, Paperback $6.95.

Available in fine bookstores and sport shops, or from;

ANDERSON WORLD, INC.

Box 336, Mountain View, CA 94042

Include $1.00 shipping and handling for each title (Maximum $3.00)